Muddy Branch

Memories of an Eastern Kentucky Coal Camp

The Northeast Coal Company store (center) *was the hub of Thealka. The company boarding house is on the right; the machine shop is on the left. Circa 1930.*

Muddy Branch

Memories of an Eastern Kentucky Coal Camp

by
Clyde Roy Pack

Jesse Stuart Foundation
Ashland, Kentucky
2002

ISBN 1-931672-10-5

Book and Jacket Design by
Designs on You!

Published by:

Jesse Stuart Foundation
1645 Winchester Avenue • P.O. Box 669
Ashland, Kentucky 41105
(606) 326-1667
JSFBOOKS.com

Table of Contents

Wilma Jean and Clyde Roy Pack

Dedication

For Wilma Jean, the love of my life, without whose encouragement and extreme patience this book could never have been completed.

And
For Todd, a son who made fatherhood a most enjoyable experience and the real writer in the family. His "Dad you ought to write that down," instigated this book.

And
For granddaughter Alison, that she may know something of her heritage.

And
For Marcy, daughter-in-law and copy editor whose proof-reading skills sped things up considerably.

And
For Dad and Mom, that their sacrifices may never be forgotten.

Preface

My first reading of Clyde Roy Pack's *Muddy Branch* convinced me of two things: first, that the manuscript should be published; and second, that Jesse Stuart Foundation should publish it. I found Clyde Roy's memoir to be honest, evocative, interesting, funny, and altogether reflective of the life we lived in the hills of Eastern Kentucky from the forties to the present. This book reads like stories from a porch swing, stories that continue to speak to me each time I read them and never fail to lead me home.

The Jesse Stuart Foundation has always been about paving the road toward home with stories, and the legacy of Stuart himself was to give voice to those of us who have little chance to be heard. Clyde Roy Pack is a home boy, absolutely. I've been knowing him since Thealka-one-through-eight fed him into Meade Memorial High School during my eighth grade year. He was best friends with my Muddy Branch cousin, Auntie Lizzie's boy, Tucker, who was the closest thing I ever had to a brother. Momma belonged to the Thealka Free Will Baptist Church where Clyde's daddy was a deacon—and Auntie Lizzie played the piano. Finally, Clyde Roy is akin to Two-Mile Creek, by marriage; he is married to Wilma Jean Penix, a Two-Mile girl I grew up with.

Muddy Branch is a memoir of Clyde Roy Pack's growing-up years in Muddy Branch coal camp in deep Eastern Kentucky.

It is the story of a boy, a place, and a time, offering a taste of a time sweet as honey, when the term "bored" had to do with something a man did with an auger.

There is in much retrospective writing—particularly concerning Appalachia—a tendency to romanticize the rural setting of the past and our parents' and grandparents' struggles with same. Conversely, the other pitfall is to engage in the kind of deconstruction that always tempts us when we look at the past from the perspective of the present. Clyde Roy has done neither. Instead, he has simply set his own truth to paper as faithfully as memory can trace it. It rings true to this Appalachian—every time.

For many outsiders the mention of Appalachia in the forties conjures up images of dense forests, cleft by dirt roads, dotted with ramshackle houses, gaunt children on sagging porches. Such a picture might be accurate, but it is incomplete. Those who were not there could not have seen how the most remote woods could abruptly give way to a trail of coal dust, a cluster of shotgun houses, a school, a church, a company store, punctuated by a tipple or two. To my growing-up eyes, the coal camp's attendant slag heap appeared as much a part of nature as the trash in our sycamore grove left by a flash flood on Two-Mile Creek. As a kid, I could not determine the distinction between a man-made mess and one caused by nature. Both creeks and coal camps were simply part of the reality of my life, one no better or worse that another. I knew that the Tug Fork of the Big Sandy River, about twenty miles to the east of Two-Mile, ran black while the Levisa Fork, some six miles west flowed brown, or sometimes green. I never thought to ask why, and it certainly never occurred to me that the color or condition of one river was somehow preferable to the other.

When Clyde Roy Pack weaves his insightful and evocative

tales of growing up in the coal camp known as Muddy Branch, he knows whereof he speaks. He spent his first eighteen years there and the spirit, feeling and atmosphere of that place in that time has clearly left its imprint. Here he has set to paper a coal camp story that creates a fresh picture of our place and our people—folks who accepted hardship, believed in the Lord, and labored long so that their kids could walk an easier path. I think you will enjoy it.

Linda Scott DeRosier, Ph.D.
Billings, MT
author of **CREEKER: A Woman's Journey**

These one-story Northeast Coal Company houses were located near the Number Three mine. The toilets were duplex, with two separate facilities under the same roof. Circa 1930.

Introduction

People look at me funny whenever I tell them I once went swimming with a dead mule. Sometimes I can almost detect the word *liar* coming from just under their breath.

Really, I can't see why there would be a big fuss about it. Although it wasn't something we did every day, it really wasn't out of the ordinary for a dead mule to be in the Number One Pond in the head of Pond Hollow. The pond was formed by slate (some called it a gob pile) dumped from the coal company's Number One mine.

Over the years, dead raccoons and 'possums were a common sight, and although the mule was a bit larger than the typical varmint we'd find, many dead animals mysteriously appeared in, then disappeared from, our ole swimming hole.

Somehow, it seemed hotter then. On the particular day in question, like every other hot summer day, along about midmorning someone yelled, "Let's go swimming!" On some days the yeller would get no takers, but on this day, within a few minutes, eight or ten of us boys, ranging in age from six to ten, were assembled on (or around) the pump rock in front of Virgil Green's house. Our number included my little brother Joe (three years my junior), Tommy "Tucker" Daniel, Paul and Wib VanHoose (brothers who lived next door to me), Jimmy and Paul Green (brothers who lived three houses below me), and Roger Ratliff. Along the way, we picked up Jimmy Spencer,

Keith Lyons and James Randell VanHoose, who lived a bit closer to our destination and were always ready for a swim.

As if by some prearranged signal, we marched single file along the narrow path around the embankment behind Foster Burton's house, picking our way through sharp gravel and sand briars. After all, school was out and our shoes had been put away for the summer, except for when we went to church or to town. The path ended behind the Thealka Free Will Baptist Church, but we continued up the railroad tracks toward the head of the hollow. The tracks ended about a quarter-mile below Lawrence Daniels' house, which was the last house in the hollow. The pond was a good quarter-mile above that. It was quite isolated, thus permitting an assortment of swimwear, or lack of same, as the case may be, and usually was.

After what seemed like an hour, but in reality could not have been more than 10 or 15 minutes, of stepping as gingerly as the man we'd seen in the newsreel walking barefooted across a bed of hot coals, we topped the slate dump. Every eye immediately fell upon the bloated brown body of the dead mule, half-covered with green flies that glistened like emeralds in the sweltering sun. It was lying practically on its back with one hind leg sticking stiffly in the air and only its head and neck were actually in the water.

Almost immediately, someone remarked rather dejectedly, "We can't go swimming."

After a long pause, someone else meekly asked, "Why?"

"'Cause, crazy, they's a dead mule in there."

"It's way up there on the other end, though."

"You crazy? You want to get germs and die?"

"Is this dog days?"

"I don't know, and what difference would it make, anyway?"

"Can germs swim?"

"Well if they can't, they can float."

"Boy, it's hotter'n a depot stove."

"It shore is. I think I got a blister on my heel, too. What do you think killed that ole mule?"

"I dunno. Old age, I guess."

"Well, shoot! How can anybody catch old-age germs?"

"Yeah, let's swim."

Looking back upon it, and remembering how hot the day was and how determined we were to swim, I believe that had the Loch Ness monster been dog-paddling back and forth, we still would have gone in.

When the first brave soul, naked as a jay bird, leaped from the four-foot-high bank, one of the smaller boys, pointing in the direction of the dead mule, yelled, "Hit's alive! Hit's alive!"

"How do you know? You crazy?"

"Hit's head moved. I swear it did!"

"That's just the waves, and besides, look at how swelled up it is."

"Yeah, and look at them flies."

"Yeah, it's dead alright. Dead as a doornail."

One at a time we boys leaped from the bank, each taking a more sizeable running go, trying to make a greater splash than the previous in an effort to cause the mule's head to dance higher and higher in the algae-green water.

"Boys, I still think we could catch germs."

"No we can't. I read in *Grit* that germs can't swim but eight feet. Just stay down here and you won't catch nothing."

That's just what we did. We simply ignored the buzzing of the flies and enjoyed yet another hot, summer day of underwater tag. Furthermore, as far as I know, none of us caught anything. But after looking in the mirror recently, I have to wonder if perhaps old-age germs can really swim.

• • •

Oh, for such days again. For the time when life was played in slow motion. When days were really 24 hours long; when Christmases and birthdays came about once every five or six years instead of every month or so; when adventure-filled summers lasted forever and life was a tad more predictable; when all I had to worry about was whether I'd be able to round up enough boys in one spot for a baseball game, gather enough pop bottles to fill a whole case to swap at the company store for an RC, nickel cake, and a chilly imp (what we called chocolate coated vanilla ice cream on a stick) or, I'd be able to catch a ride to town for the Saturday matinees, although I really didn't mind walking.

Even as I hunted for a horse hair in what was at one time the Northeast Coal Company's dairy barn (which had long since become a shelter for horses, too) so I could place it under a big rock in the creek to see if it really would, as prevailing rumor in the neighborhood promised, turn into a snake, I think I knew that with my youth came a certain degree of protective innocence. It was Dad and Mom's responsibility to be concerned about paying the rent, buying the groceries, and supplying me with a new tablet and pencils when school started. It was up to them to worry about the war, about my older brothers who were fighting in it.

As a coal-camp kid I hardly knew the difference between a pick and a shovel and only existed on the fringe of reality, hearing bits and pieces of conversations about the United Mine Workers Association and its president John L. Lewis, company layoffs, fatal accidents at the mines, and widows and orphans who needed help from church funds.

Obviously, one thing that makes those days of my seemingly

endless childhood so appealing is the simple fact that I had my youth then and had tons of time to do whatever it was I wanted to do.

In the opening paragraphs of his best-selling, *Angela's Ashes*, Frank McCourt described his childhood in Ireland as being miserable. Mine was not. My father was neither drunken nor shiftless and my mother was not depressed. This memoir might even be considered an antithesis to McCourt's. Even though my family had little in terms of material goods, I wish everybody could have experienced a childhood like mine.

• • •

So, references to any person, place, or thing from my past should be regarded as nothing more than memories. I will admit to changing some names here and there because the last thing I would want to do is cause embarrassment to certain individuals.

All the families in Muddy Branch just seemed to be trying to make it from one day to the next, feeding and clothing their children, who were plentiful, and seeing that they got as good an education as possible. Some succeeded, some didn't.

By and large, though, as a group, we coal-camp kids didn't fare too badly. Of the list of boys and girls mentioned in these pages, several, including me, grew up to be teachers. One ended up an Army officer, another a county judge-executive. Our neighborhood also produced a preacher, a dentist, a chemist, several firemen, and of course, a coal miner or two. To my knowledge, as hard as it is to believe, none of us became reprobates.

The older I've gotten, the more I've come to appreciate how (and where) I grew up. That's not to suggest that I turned out perfectly or that my parents didn't make mistakes. Neither am I suggesting that the 1940s were the best years in history to be a kid, nor that living in an Eastern Kentucky coal camp was a Utopian existence.

It's just that every time I read a newspaper or watch the evening news on TV, I realize how lucky I was to have been a kid living in what seemed to be a normal society and having normal parents.

Dad worked in the mines and Mom stayed home. I had six brothers and sisters, and even though we were poor—which wasn't really all that big a deal since we didn't know it until we were grown and LBJ came and declared war on our poverty—I never in my life went to bed hungry.

I appreciate the fact that I felt secure living in a coal camp, although even in the forties I knew of an occasional alcoholic and other people who were viewed as somewhat less than model citizens.They were the exception, not the rule; their behavior was frowned upon, not accepted. People didn't say, "These are modern times. Leave them alone."

The contrast between then and now is indeed stark, because we're talking about a time when it was considered to be against the law for two unmarried people of the opposite sex to "live together" (we referred to it as "shacking up."); when same-sex marriages would have been akin to the ultimate sin; when surrogate motherhood and test-tube babies were so far in the future they weren't even acceptable as fiction. These days of drive-by shootings and abortion on demand make times back then look as innocent as an all-day gospel sing with dinner on the ground.

So, even at the expense of many wrinkles, a few gray hairs, and more than a few aches and pains, I'm glad I'm a product of then instead of now.

As anyone who ever lived in one can attest, a coal camp back then provided a different way of life regardless of what name appeared over the post office door. That comes as no surprise, though, because the industry that spawned those communities was as unique and intriguing as any plot ever devised in a work of fiction. Unlikely heroes whose brave deeds were heralded, then quickly forgotten, popped up on a near-daily basis as they dragged to daylight the victims of those ever-present accidents which mining techniques of the day afforded.

Ironically, most of the time these Eastern Kentucky mountains seemed perfectly benign. But whether appearing completely sterile after a three-inch blanket of new-fallen snow, or in autumn, resembling a grandmother's patch-work quilt stitched with every bright color her rag bag could provide, our hills often were nothing more than well-camouflaged traps set to maim or even snatch the breath from, and in some cases entomb forever, those brave enough to crawl into their depths.

The children of the miners who died beneath these hills, as well as those whose daddies were lucky enough to have survived long enough to have their lungs eaten away by years of accumulating rock dust (officially diagnosed as silicosis, but better known as "black lung"), sprang from an environment that absolutely demanded they be as tough as seasoned stove wood. And, together they fought any outsider, usually defined as anyone from another hollow or from town, who threatened their territory.

Children of an industry that sometimes forced its participants to donate body parts, from single digits to entire limbs became both physically and mentally hardened. They eventually fought wars on foreign soil, many returning to seek employment themselves on job sites their fathers vowed their children would never visit.

Beginning in the 1950s, many of the big mining companies, thinking they'd taken enough, left Eastern Kentucky. What remained was a hardy generation of survivors, coal miners' kids, who know the meaning of hard work; who are doing whatever is necessary to ensure a better life for their own children; and who will forever appreciate the sacrifices of parents who struggled in an industry that demanded so much.

• • •

References to Muddy Branch, or Thealka, in the following pages are absolutely *not* to be taken as an historical account of how things were when I was growing up there in the forties and fifties. I do not claim to be an historian, at least not to the point where I spent hours poring over courthouse records or examining various ancient publications, and I was enjoying myself far too much to take notes as I went along. Neither can I promise 100 percent accuracy regarding some of the things that happened to me. After a lifetime, it's hard to know the difference in what I remember and what I remember hearing from Dad and Mom and all my older brothers and sisters.

But this book is not about me. It is a tale of a group of hardy, God-fearing people who occupied this community when I was growing up there. It is my desire to convey their language, customs and strong faith so that others may know who they were and the contributions they made to our society.

CHAPTER I

Hidden in the Hills

My father was not only a coal miner, but also a dyed-in-the-wool Free Will Baptist who believed that he and every member of his family needed to occupy a pew every time the church doors were opened. Consequently, I was scrubbed behind the ears, placed in clean bibbed overalls, marched into Sunday School, and taught to believe the Bible, as one old preacher said, "...from Genesis to the maps."

"Honesty is the best policy" and "Do unto others," were tattooed on my brain by adults who taught by example.

Once when a man, in the dead of night, sneaked into our smokehouse and stole a whole ham that my father had been curing, Dad discovered his identity.

He also knew that the thief had a whole houseful of kids. And what the thief didn't know was that had he only asked for the ham, not only would Dad have given it to him, he probably would have even sliced it.

I overheard the end of a conversation about a later confrontation between Dad and the thief.

Mom: "And what did you say, Willie?"

Dad: "I just asked him if he had a ham sandwich in his bucket."

Mom: "And what did he say?"

Dad: "Not a word. Not a word."

That exchange probably said as much about the kind of man my father was as anything else. I'm sure he got a great deal of satisfaction from knowing the thief's children were being fed, and an equal amount of satisfaction in letting the thief know, "I gotcha!"

"I want to live every day so I can sleep every night," he'd say.

It was years before I knew what that meant.

Of course, not all the people who lived in the camp shared my father's views.

So although *Peyton Place* was yet to be a best seller, and even though conversations of a sexual nature did not appear on daytime TV, there were constant rumors of infidelity in the neighborhood. These were discussed in hushed tones almost, but not quite out of earshot of the youngsters. *Infidelity* is *my* word. Such subjects were expressed in more colorful colloquialisms in those days. I never heard the word "prostitute." A married woman who was sleeping around was simply a "whore" or a "rip." As a matter of fact, those terms were used for any woman who was sleeping around, whether she was married or not.

And, although he wasn't as loveable as Andy Griffith's pal Otis Campbell, nor as obnoxious as comedian Foster Brooks, we even had our designated neighborhood drunk. Later in these pages I'll explain how he nearly caused me to start drinking, too.

So in most aspects, people then were pretty much like people are now. It's just that living in the kind of close proximity that only a mining camp could afford—sharing similar living quarters (a yellow Northeast Coal Company house), the same religious persuasion (Free Will Baptist), and identical financial burdens because everybody was equally poor and paid for groceries with credit drawn at the company store—neighbors grew closer than neighbors do now.

And yes, despite the fact that many of the folks I grew up with (and around) all my life choose now to deny it, we were just a big bunch of Eastern Kentucky hillbillies. It really aggravates me the way some folks react to being tagged "backwoodsey."

I'm convinced that most of the grievous wounds we've suffered over the years in regard to our "hillbilly" image have been self-inflicted, anyway.

I'm not ashamed to admit that when I grew up in a coal camp I rarely wore shoes in the summertime. But I had them if I'd wanted to wear them. And socks, too, for that matter. I know that. If outsiders fail to realize that, then they're the ignorant ones, not me.

I'll even admit to owning both a guitar and a dulcimer; to enjoying the music of George Jones and Bluegrass balladeer Hylo Brown; and to watching as many Andy Griffith reruns as I can. I even laugh sometimes at Jeff Foxworthy's "You know you're a Redneck when..." jokes, and would rather be in the audience at the Grand Ole Opry than at a performance of the three tenors.

What we're going to have to do is stop taking it personally when the national media distorts our reality. Like the *48 Hours* presentation on CBS-TV back in 1989—the one about a place called Muddy Gut that I think made all Kentuckians look impoverished.

The show's introduction went something like this:

"There is another America hidden in the hills of Appalachia—a disturbing journey to a world apart," the announcer (probably Dan Rather) said. *"Back in the hills of Kentucky, you'll find some of the poorest places in America. This is where Washington waged a war on poverty and lost."*

My suggestion would be a sequel with the narrator saying: *"There is another America hidden in Appalachia's hills—a disturbing journey for those who watch too much TV; for those expecting to round the next bend and be confronted by Jethro, Jed and Ellie Mae; for those who might suffer a heart attack if they meet kids who don't have lice and rickets and who wear shoes—Nikes, no less."*

• • •

Yes, we do indeed live in another world; I for one am glad we do, and, I might just have stumbled onto the reason we're here.

As my wife Wilma Jean and I drove along Route 40 on a recent January afternoon, enjoying nature in all its black-and-white stark nakedness, and waiting impatiently for another genuine dogwood spring and a shady sycamore summer, our conversation turned to our ancestors.

"Why," she mused, "do you think they decided to settle here?"

While neither of us is into genealogy, and, in truth, had no clue as to the answer to that question, we each offered our hastily-thought-out theory as to why our great-great-grandfathers didn't go farther south or west or, heaven forbid, north. But, as would be expected, neither of us managed to convince the other that our ideas had much merit.

Then, a few weeks later, and quite by accident, I stumbled upon a piece of writing by Kiowa poet N. Scott Momaday, who, speaking of the American West, wrote, "It is a landscape that has to be seen to be believed, and may have to be believed to be seen."

"Perhaps that's it," I thought. "Maybe our ancestors saw,

and believed, in Eastern Kentucky. Perhaps as they endured the hardships that four genuine seasons forced upon their pioneer families, they came to believe in the land they saw."

Those of us whose innermost lives are inextricably linked to the ruggedness of the hills, should instead of grumbling about image and some silly names that others are calling us, be remembering that our forefathers pulled their very livelihood from beneath the top layers and deep bowels of this mountainous terrain.

We should feel fortunate to have come from a people who saw a cold, black January night while believing in a bright, new April morning.

We're what we are now because *then* they had patience, as well as dreams that extended far beyond the practical and which, every once in a while, did indeed come true.

• • •

One of the most obvious things that sets us apart from everybody else is the way we talk. Words and phrases that are common to us apparently seem foreign to someone from "off." Unfortunately, to combat *their* lack of knowledge of our uniqueness, some outsiders try to degrade *us* because *they* aren't smart enough to know what it is *we're* saying.

For the benefit of those not familiar with our dialect, here are a few pieces of terminology with which I grew up, defined and used correctly in a sentence. Of course, not all Eastern Kentuckians talk this way on all occasions.

• **Pwerently** (one of Mom's favorite words): not really. He's *pwerently* going to give her a big diamond for Christmas.

- **Hind part afore**: backward. He put his pants on *hind part afore*.
- **Might nigh**: almost. Jake *might nigh* shot his own cow.
- **Pert neer** (pretty near): might nigh. Jake *pert neer* shot his own cow.
- **Fair to middlin'**: doing okay. "How ya doing?" "Oh, I'm *fair to middlin'*, I guess. How 'bout yourself?"
- **Heavy set**: overweight. That lady sure is *heavy set*. (This was a favorite term of my dad's. He absolutely refused to say that someone was *fat*.)
- **Flashy** (fleshy): heavy set. That lady is kind of *flashy*.
- **Big-boned**: flashy. She's so *big-boned* she can't get through that door.
- **Raisin' Cain**: drinking and swarpin'. Those boys are sure *raisin' Cain* tonight.
- **Swarpin'**: running around at night and raising Cain with a bunch of wild boys, but with something in mind a bit more sinister than just drinking and usually having something to do with girls. Drinking's bad, but that *swarpin'* will absolutely kill you.
- **Here lately**: recently. I haven't been feeling too good *here lately*.
- **Here while back**: in the not too distant past. She broke her arm *here while back*.
- **Holler**: yell. "Did you *holler* at me?"
- **Holler**: having nothing inside. He's got a *holler* head.
- **Holler**: the valley between two hills. I live over in the next *holler*.
- **Fer piece**: a great distance. I live a *fer piece* up the holler.

- **Smidgen**: a measurement in cooking. Add a *smidgen* of salt to the recipe.
- **Smack dab**: exactly in the middle. She hit him *smack dab* between the eyes.
- **Plumb blank**: smack dab. She hit him *plumb blank* between the eyes.
- **Boggin**: a cap worn in the wintertime. Somebody stole my *boggin*. (Also sometimes referred to as a day cap.)
- **Shine** (short for moonshine): an illegal alcoholic beverage that's still made. Let's get the fire going and heat the kettle and make us some more *shine*.
- **Shine**: disturbance. He was very upset and cut the biggest *shine* you ever saw.
- **Coal gon**: A long railroad car with no top used for hauling coal. I told you boys not to be climbing on those *coal gons*.
- **Chilly imp**: Ice cream on a stick; vanilla on the inside with a chocolate coating. You had to eat a *chilly imp* real fast in the summertime.
- **Press**: What city folks call a closet. I keep all my important papers in a cigar box on the top shelf of the *press*.
- **Blar**: Those sharp, sticky things on blackberry vines. The reason I'm all scratched up is because I've been in the *blar* patch.
- **Safe**: A kitchen cabinet. Dad kept his billfold on top of the safe.
- **Briggidy**: How you were not supposed to act when you had company. Now remember, when the preacher gets here, don't start acting *briggidy*.
- **Show out**: to act briggidy. Little Cecil is trying to *show out*.

- **Biddy drownder**: An extremely hard rain, somewhat akin to a frog strangler. Boy, this is a regular *biddy drownder*, ain't it?

- **Bug winding** (with *winding* pronounced like winding a watch): A great distance. If he says one more word to me, I'm going to knock him a *bug winding*.

- **Finger plaster**: What some people called a Band-Aid. Put a *finger plaster* on it. You'll be all right.

- **Miner's strawberries**: Another name for soup (pinto) beans. Mom's fixing *miner's strawberries* for supper.

- **Poke**: A paper sack. We carried groceries in a *poke*.

- **Poke**: A type of wild green that Mom picked every spring. I enjoy a good mess (when there's enough for everybody who eats) of *poke*.

- **Shuck beans**: Green beans threaded and dried. A good mess of *shuck beans* makes a mighty tasty meal.

- **Leather britches**: Another name for shuck beans. Got any more of them *leather britches* left, Mom?

- **Roshineers** (roasting ears): Corn on the cob. I love butter on my *roshineers*.

CHAPTER II

A Coal Camp Was a Coal Camp

As we kids frittered away our summers, we gave no thought to how our parents came to live in a coal camp. After all, we were only kids and the world apart from ours, either past or present, didn't hold any significance in our lives.

I was well into adulthood before I'd ever heard of Morris Williams, Carl Metzger and A.D.W. Smith, but according to documents given me once by long-time Northeast employee Theodore Miller, it was they who sat down in Philadelphia in 1906 and signed the papers that officially formed the Northeast Coal Company. They obviously felt secure in the knowledge that the mountains were full of coal and that Eastern Kentuckians would devote their lives to removing it. What they probably didn't realize, though, was that an ordinary business transaction was in fact a birthing, slapping life into Thealka, another small community like the many others that would come to dot the map from one end of Appalachia to the other.

During the first half of the 20th century, communities like Thealka, in Johnson County, Kentucky, became all things to all people who lived in them, and at the same time, became a microcosm of America herself.

Geographically, Thealka was less than two miles northeast of Paintsville, the county seat. The closest big towns were Huntington, West Virginia, around 60 miles to the northeast, and

Lexington, Kentucky, which was about twice that far to the northwest.

But Thealka was at once wholly American, and yet, uniquely Eastern Kentucky. It existed in sort of a social paradox, its inhabitants basking in the security of guaranteed employment during hard times, at the very least on a part-time basis, yet facing daily dread that the wages earned would not be sufficient to feed and clothe the families. Accompanying this was the ever-present, yet unspoken, threat of disaster that early mining techniques provided. Dad's younger brother Steve was killed in the mines in the early 1940s, and Dad himself was mashed up by roof falls a couple of times and had left the pinky finger of his left hand somewhere in the vast darkness of a Northeast shaft after a rusty cog cleanly sliced it from his hand. My brother Ernest wore a speckled, blue-tattoo scar over his right eye for the rest of his life after a roof fall in a Breathitt County mine in the late 1950s crushed his hard hat and came close to doing the same to his skull.

During the Depression and war years, folks in Thealka went about their daily chores, doing what was necessary to pull the coal from the ground and strength from each other. They sent their daddies to the mines and their sons and daughters (as was the case for Irene Dale, our next-door neighbor) to war, and in both cases, welcomed home those who returned and grieved eternally those who didn't.

Then, in the 1950s, almost in unison, mines all over Eastern Kentucky began closing. T-rails rusted and weeds grew between the cross ties of the miles of railroad tracks that snaked along the creek beds and hillsides.

Miners with young families began loading their belongings into pickup trucks and heading north to the unfamiliar geography of Dayton, Detroit and Wabash, Indiana, where my brother

Ernest moved his family. The hands that once dug coal now molded tires and shaped bumpers, and some of these families never returned.

In 1955 Dad was 55 years old, so he opted to stay put. He worked in various small, privately owned truck mines, which were tiny, non-union, low-paying mines that delivered their coal by trucks instead of rail like larger operations did.

Dad ended up buying and remodeling one of the old two-story company houses. It was the first house that Dad or Mom had ever lived in that had indoor plumbing. He lived out his days on a small miner's pension and the black lung check he began drawing in 1964. He died from black lung in 1969 and Mom died of cancer in 1976 while living with my older sister Mary Jean in Moultrie, Georgia.

• • •

The bard of Avon posed this question: "What's in a name?"

You can call the community in which I was reared Muddy Branch. You can call it Society Row or Silk Stocking Row or Well Hollow or Number One. You can refer to it as Boyd Branch, Number Three, Concord or Rock House. Call it what you may, though, Thealka is Thealka and the only place in the world where I was born. Throughout this book, just keep in mind that a reference to any of the above is still a reference to Thealka.

Actually, with all its many creeks and hollows, there is, if you care to ferret it out, a degree of logic in how one little place in the middle of Eastern Kentucky could be called so many things. One theory as to how it came to be called Thealka (which someone once suggested sounded Indian, but it's not) regarded a river boat that ran aground at about the turn of the last century in the Levisa Fork of the Big Sandy River near

Greentown. (Greentown is yet another part of Thealka, and sits next to the river on Route 581, along the eastern border of Paintsville.) The name of the boat was *The Alka*, and people began referring to that part of the county as "...down there where the Alka is."

I suppose, however, the most prevalent theory, involving that same boat, is that a sign painter messed up the spacing and ran the two words together, thus making the boat's name *TheAlka*.

The riverboat The Alka, *circa 1900.*

The Alka was named after the wife of coal baron John C. C. Mayo who, depending upon which historian you choose to believe, was either a saint or a scoundrel.

Muddy Branch was what people called the main creek that ran through the neighborhood, because it usually was. Society Row and Silk Stocking Row were one and the same, again depending upon who was talking. The houses were bigger in this part of the camp and were, most likely, considered a bit fancier. They were located just above the company store in the vicinity of the Free Will Baptist Church. Boyd Branch, supposedly named after an early family who lived there, is what they called the little creek that ran through that particular part of the community.

Well Hollow got its name because there were several gas wells (and you could smell them for miles) scattered throughout the area. Northeast's Number One Mine and tipple, which closed in 1937, were located in a little hollow nearby, as was the aforementioned pond in which we swam.

The company's Number Two mine, which was closed long before my time, had been located at Concord. To reach Concord, we had to turn right-handed immediately after crossing the railroad tracks at Greentown. Residents of the community say that Concord got its name from the little Concord United Baptist Church that sat at the foot of the hill as you entered the community. No one ever said how the church got *its* name.

Concord Road, being rather isolated, was reportedly a perfect place for young lovers (and old lechers) to park late at night. I really don't know much about that, but it was a good place for young boys on bicycles to gather along about dark. Concord Road provided a perfect view of the Cain Auto Theatre and many's the night we'd watch the cartoon (without sound, of course) from that particular vantage point.

To get to Rock House you turned right just after you passed the Thealka Post Office, which sat on an embankment on the left side of the road just on the Muddy Branch side of the Greentown railroad tracks. A narrow gravel road about a mile long snaked its way up the hollow and over the hill into the little community. Local lore explains that Rock House got its name because there were once two red brick buildings that sat at the mouth of the hollow near the community's entrance. I often wondered why they didn't call it Brick House.

Although Rock House was not as densely populated as other parts of Thealka, there was a time when more than two dozen boys and girls (mostly Castles and Prestons) walked across that hill every morning to go to school at Muddy Branch. Their walk to school was probably three times longer than mine. Some of them caught the bus to Meade Memorial High School, as did I. Meade Memorial was at Williamsport, about seven or eight miles east on Route 40.

Continuing toward Tutor Key on Route 581, the next neighborhood was often referred to as Number Three because Northeast's Number Three Mine was located there. This mine was the last of the Northeast operations to go, closing in 1957.

As Shakespeare said, "A rose by any other name would smell as sweet."

The Northeast Coal Company's No. 3 tipple in Thealka, circa 1935.

So, I suppose it doesn't really matter what you call this dusty little Johnson County coal camp, with its rows of yellow houses, winding creeks and miles of railroad tracks. It's perhaps not as well known as Van Lear, Loretta Lynn's birthplace, which is in the same county (about five or six miles southeast of Thealka, as the crow flies), but to those who grew up there, when you mention Thealka these days, you're speaking not only of a place, but also a time. A time that can never again be as it used to be, except in memories.

When I enrolled in Eastern Kentucky State College in 1957, I told everybody I was from Paintsville instead of Muddy Branch or Thealka. I guess I could have been accused of acting above my raisin', but at the same time, I didn't want to risk the inevitable question, "Where?," and be labeled a hick from the sticks. Not that I didn't propagate that notion every time I opened my mouth to speak. To me a *window* was a *winder*, and *chance* was *chanch*. I had to repeat myself a lot in those days.

If I suggested we roll down the winder of the car someone would laugh and ask what a winder was. I'd laugh along with them, but for the life of me I couldn't see why they thought it was funny.

Anyway, it wasn't until many years had passed that I became embarrassed about denying my heritage. As I got older, I realized that place names in Eastern Kentucky merely add to our uniqueness. In this county alone we have communities called Meally, Kerz, Whippoorwill and Chestnut.

• • •

During the daytime, by paying attention to the pugged noses, buck teeth, red hair and other general characteristics of the children who straddled ridey bobs made by planks stuck through the horizontal slats of the wooden fence, local residents could pretty much tell what family lived where. That is, of course, if all the above were stationed in front of their own dwellings, which more often than not, they weren't.

To the less frequent visitor, however, and especially at night, and even more especially if one were as drunk as a skunk, all the houses in Society Row looked exactly the same. So much so, in fact, that if a person weren't familiar with the territory, he could easily walk through the front door of one house, thinking it belonged to another...which had been known to happen on more than one occasion. I remember Mom telling about how some drunk man had accidentally walked in on old Mrs. Skeens while she was sweeping her kitchen and she about beat him to death with her broom handle before he could escape. I never heard whether he finally got to his intended destination.

Me, Dad, Joe and Mom in 1949. This view provides a good look at the front of the two-story houses in Society Row.

The houses in Society Row had neither house numbers, individual landscaping nor any variations whatsoever, since each house was constructed from the same plan. Imagine placing three large building blocks end-to-end to represent the downstairs. Now, place two more blocks exactly over the first two for the two upstairs rooms. Cover them with a slanted roof, add a front porch and you've got a Northeast Coal Company two-story house. Put a smaller block out back at a distance representing 20 or 30 yards, and you've added a bathroom.

After all my older siblings had moved out, leaving only little brother Joe and me, we used the downstairs room nearest the front porch as a living room, although that's not what we called it. We simply referred to it as the front room. We had a couch and chairs and end tables, but for many of the homes in Society Row, especially if they housed large families, this was just another bedroom.

Regardless of its desired function, the middle room was always referred to as the middle room and, depending on the size of the family who lived there, had a variety of uses. Most of the families in

This photo of my sister, Mary Jean, and our niece, Erna Jean, affords a good view of the backside of the community.

Muddy Branch were large in those days, so more often than not, this was another bedroom, just like at our house.

Our problem, though, was that this was the room in which Mom and Dad slept. The staircase was in this room, too, and when anybody came in late at night, they had to walk right by Mom and Dad's bed to get upstairs to theirs. Another problem with these particular sleeping arrangements was that when Dad was on the day shift, he had to get up at 4:30 in the morning, so he went to bed very early. When he'd grab the cat and throw it out the back door, it meant quietness would prevail for the rest of the night. So, off would go the radio, and up the stairs Joe and I would go. If we weren't really sleepy, we'd read funny books for a while.

The use of the room at the back of the house was definitely consistent throughout the neighborhood: it was the kitchen. At our house, there was always something cooking in the kitchen, literally, and the aroma of cornbread baking, bacon frying or soupbeans cooking always permeated the air. Mom wasn't much of a cake baker, but she baked a lot of pies and cobblers, and I'll never forget the smells in her kitchen.

The kitchen table was where Joe and I did our homework, which was usually no more than eight or ten arithmetic problems or making a few sentences from the next day's spelling words.

From the kitchen, one stepped out onto the back porch, which, more likely than not, held the family Maytag washer. Even during the coldest days of winter, we kept our washer out there and Mom would just roll it inside when she did the weekly wash. Dad had dug a nice big hole in the little creek that ran next to our yard and Joe and I, with a long-handled cooker, would bail water in buckets to fill up two number-two wash tubs so mom could wash our clothes. In the summertime,

if the creek was dry, we'd carry the water from the neighborhood pump. And, of course, sometimes there'd be an ample
supply of rain water collected from two tubs that were always
sitting beneath the drip of the house.

The two rooms upstairs were always used as bedrooms, and
again, depending upon the size of the family, each contained
one to three beds. Thank goodness I didn't snore then like
Wilma Jean says I do now, or I'd likely have been sleeping on
the back porch with the cat, which curled up on a pile of old
rags under the Maytag. I can't remember when we didn't have
a cat.

I guess the color of these houses could have been called
"bituminous yellow" for I suspect they achieved their particular hue as a result of the coal dust that settled from the nearby
tipple. In all my years as an art student and teacher, I was never,
even by accident, able to duplicate that exact shade of yellow.

The house's interiors featured plastered walls and were left
to the artistic tastes, or lack of same, of the inhabitants. I'll never
forget the color that one family painted their downstairs rooms.
Montgomery Ward (everything the company store didn't have,
"Monkey" Ward did) must have run a sale on this color, because
the family painted the walls of all three rooms a blistering pink.

These folks had no kids my age, so I had never been invited
inside this particular home and had only viewed it from the
vantage of the front porch. But, when this family moved out, a
few of us raised a kitchen window, as was the custom, and went
inside, hoping those who had just vacated the premises had
left something useful lying around: perhaps a stack of old funny
books or maybe an old catcher's mitt. I can't remember anything of that nature being discovered, but we did discover that
when they had painted, they hadn't moved a single stick of
furniture. Instead, they had just painted around everything,

even the large picture of Jesus praying in the Garden that had been visible from the front porch and had hung in an oval frame above their couch.

But to be perfectly honest, what I remember most about the houses are the folks who lived in them. Although there was constant bickering among the kids, a certain prevailing calm seemed to exist in the community. It was as if each family knew it was somehow dependent upon the other, like we were all in this thing together.

• • •

When I was growing up in Muddy Branch, I not only knew where every family lived, but I also knew all their children and most of their ages. It wasn't because I was nosy, either. I think it was simply because everybody had a front porch. Furthermore, every one of them had a swing.

During the day, it was unthinkable, whether you were a kid or an adult, to walk by someone sitting in their swing without exchanging a word or two. At night, especially in the summertime, folks would sit on their front porches until way up into the night, until the cool air had chased away the heat of day so they could sleep.

While they sat, they talked—not only to each other, but also from porch to porch. Thanks to the front porch, folks shared a friendship and camaraderie that is just impossible to attain in today's world. Folks shared one another's happiness, as well as those inevitable moments of tragedy. It was really worth something to know that in a time of need, help was just as close as your nearest neighbor's front porch.

Oh, I'm sure that many folks today still have front porches, and I'm sure that some of them use them the way they were meant to be used. But, by and large, especially in newly constructed homes, front porches are practically non-existent. I'm afraid that those that are built, are built for show. And if there are any today that are actually sat upon, there's likely a privacy fence to keep people from seeing who's sitting.

I suspect we'd be a better society if Congress would pass a law requiring all houses to have front porches, with wooden swings.

• • •

The aforementioned "little block out back" was simply called the toilet. I mention this because from time to time I run into those with whom I shared my childhood and some want to refer to it as "the privy" or "the outhouse." Baloney. It was simply a plain old smelly toilet, furnished and maintained by the Northeast Coal Company, and no, its door was not adorned with a quarter moon like the one in Lil' Abner's Dog Patch.

Strangely enough, not only did these little four-by-four, roughly hewn, unpainted structures serve their usual and expected purposes, but for me at least, they also became sort of a yardstick, measuring the social status of the families whose back doors were tied to them by well-worn paths.

As a boy playing cowboys and Indians or hunting pop bottles up and down the back lane, and even though I knew Mom would wear me out if she ever found out, I had the occasion to visit practically every one of these little rest stops at least once. Thus, the first hint of just how far up the social ladder the folks upon whose throne I sat, or stood before, had climbed, had nothing to do with fancy gold faucets and stuff. Instead it pertained to the choice of reading material they made available. For example, if I were forced to sit and read the *United Mine Workers Journal* or the Montgomery Ward or Sears and Roebuck catalog, I knew that these people were on about the same social scale as my family.

Those a rung or two higher would furnish me with old copies of the *Grit*, and the real uppity-ups would provide me with the latest issue of *Progressive Farmer*. The slogan, "Please don't squeeze my Charmin," was yet to be invented.

Men from Northeast would come three or four times a year, dig a new hole and move the toilets. This always drew a crowd of curious ten-year-old boys who were always warned (needlessly, I might add) to "stand way back."

One tale that made the rounds just about every time a toilet was moved involved Ambrose Castle's cow. Apparently, on one occasion in the not-too-distant past, the men from Northeast hadn't filled the hole completely, or maybe the dirt had just been soft. Regardless of why it happened, though, it happened. One night during a prayer meeting at the home of Milt Ratliff, the cow, which had apparently strayed from where it had been penned up for the night, walked into his recently-filled toilet hole and sank up to her udder. She raised the whole neighborhood with her bawling and it took four grown men with a strong rope (and stronger stomachs) to pull her out. Harkless O'Bryant, who was a nephew of Ambrose and Ellen Castle and who lived with them, had to take the cow to the creek in the dead of night and wash her off.

Since the toilets merely sat, unanchored, on large concrete slabs, the popularity of the residents whose houses they adjoined was often reflected on Halloween night. That's when some of those old mean boys, after everyone else had all gone to bed, would make their rounds and turn over the toilets of everyone they didn't particularly like. Of course, no real harm was done because at the time, they were unoccupied, and next morning, here'd come the men from Northeast to set them upright again. It was quite a sight, though, to stand in the head of Society Row and by dawn's early light see, like so many fallen soldiers, every other toilet lying on its side.

While many of us spend a good deal of time these days reminiscing about the "good ole days," I sometimes wonder why we never give much thought to the lack of plumbing we experienced back then. It was no fun to use the old slop jar or get dressed, complete with boots and overcoat, and tramp out into a winter night at three in the morning in 10-degree weather. Those were our options, though, and all I know is that having no indoor plumbing was a way of life for us then, and we never gave it a second thought. Well, almost never.

• • •

It would be several years before indoor plumbing existed for us. Consequently, our drinking water came from two pumps, one located in the upper end of the camp, the other in the lower. Each pump served a dozen or so families and came equipped with a long handle and a spout on which we could hang our water buckets. The pumps sat on large concrete slabs about five feet square that came to be known as "pump rocks."

The pump rocks were more than just places to set the pumps, however. They also became places of rendezvous for us kids, as well as an ever-flowing fountain of gossip for the adults, especially the older girls and women.

Now, I'm not saying there was anything wrong with that. As a matter of fact, I suspect it was all quite natural. After all, these ladies didn't have Oprah or those inquiring-mind tabloids available. They did have the *Grit*, but that news was at least a week old. So all they had, really, was Gabriel Heatter and his radio broadcasts, and while his news was almost always optimistic, even informative, it was not the least bit juicy.

So, pump rock sessions thus became a source of news *and* entertainment. Words were seldom spoken louder than a whisper, or louder than was necessary to be heard over the metal-against-metal shriek of the pump handle as the ladies of Society Row filled their buckets with water and their heads with all the latest news. It was nearly as if the pump rock became a sacred place, almost church-like, and the soft whispers of conversation came to resemble some sort of religious ritual.

Being centrally located, the pump rock was also a place of rendezvous and on Saturday mornings, especially in the summertime, a bunch of us boys would gather there and walk to Paintsville for the Saturday matinees at the Sipp (on Main Street) and the Royal (on Second Street). We, no doubt, looked like a small army as, on those days we couldn't catch a ride (we didn't hitch-hike, but we certainly didn't turn anybody down if they stopped and offered us a lift), we'd take the railroad tracks up through Greentown, crawl through the fence behind Bill Pigg's, then follow Route 40 on into town. It wasn't more than a mile or two, but on those hot, muggy dog-day Saturday mornings, it seemed longer.

Every once in a while, we'd also walk to the show on Saturday night. Of course, it'd be daylight when we'd go, but by the time the show was over, it'd be good and dark. On the way out of town, we'd stop at Raymond Brugh's pool room on Main Street and buy us each a big Roi-Tan cigar for a nickel, if we had managed to save one. We'd feel ten feet tall and bullet-proof as we walked home and discussed that week's episode of "Undersea Kingdom." It was the general consensus that Crash Corrigan would probably be okay, but for the life of us, we couldn't see how.

Walking home at night wasn't all that bad as long as we were still in the lights of town. Walking the railroad tracks through

Greentown, though, was another matter, especially when someone would declare his bravery by saying that he absolutely did not believe that the stretch of tracks between the Thealka post office and the company store was haunted and that there was no way a ghost with no head could really chase anybody. We'd usually run that stretch, but not because we were scared. Somebody would yell, "Race ya," and not one of us could resist a challenge.

Looking back, I also think that there was a bit more to our traveling in large numbers than just our desire for companionship, our fear of headless ghosts and our love for Roy Rogers, Gene Autry and Lash Larue. There was also the dreaded, but seldom spoken of, thought of confrontation with various other groups our age from town. Although we never had an ill word with any of them, the Turkey Knobbers and Bristle Buckers, I later learned these two groups of kids from two particular neighborhoods within the Paintsville city limits, were at constant war with each other, and at least in our minds, were always a threat to us.

CHAPTER III

The H.S. Howes Community School

After more than 50 years I can still remember, though I'd never have admitted it to my peers at the time, how much I looked forward to walking into the classroom on the first day of school after a long, hot summer of doing as little as possible in the way of usefulness. Of course, catching waterdogs and crawdads and swimming in the Number One Pond at every opportunity, probably did seem like useful, even absolutely necessary, activities at the time.

The aroma of freshly oiled floors mixed with the scent of new crayons and the stale odor of textbooks being taken from boxes long stored and stacked in some musty corner all summer, is still vivid to me. It was exciting to open each newly assigned textbook and discover who had used it last year...and the year before that. Some previous owners of the arithmetic books were most helpful and had penciled in answers to some of the more difficult problems. It never occurred to me that some of them could have been wrong.

I can also remember lying awake the night before the first day of school each year worrying that my new teacher would be some sort of horrible monster. Such concern was totally unfounded, however, because when I was in grade school I never once had a teacher I didn't like.

The first principal I ever had was Garfield Chandler, a balding, slightly heavy-set gentleman who always dressed in a dark suit with a broad tie and reminded me of a preacher. He carried a new store-bought paddle that I never once saw him use except in fun. He would walk up beside you and pop you one with a behind-the-back swat, then stand looking innocently ahead as if nothing ever happened. It was rumored that he had an electric paddle in his office, but to my knowledge, no one ever actually saw it.

Miss Angie Ward taught me in both first and second grades. All I remember about her was that she was a small woman and very kind. She must have been a good teacher because I had no trouble when I moved up to third grade. She was teaching first grade at Paintsville Elementary many years later when I started teaching there in 1967, but didn't seem impressed that one of her pupils had grown up to be a teacher. As a matter of fact, I'm not sure she even remembered me.

Flora Adams was my teacher in the third and fourth grades.

Third-and fourth-grade classes were in the same room and my teacher was Mrs. Flora Adams. She only had one full arm (her left arm ended at her elbow, the result of falling from a tree when she was a child), but that didn't keep her from applying the "board of education," as she called it, to the seat of my pants whenever I needed it. At first I felt sorry for her, what with her being disabled and all. But I soon learned that she was as capable as anybody else, and when she'd place that stub in the small of my back as she tanned my bottom with her right hand, I began to pity myself more than I did her. I think the worse thrashing she ever gave me was when she intercepted a love note I'd written to Frankie Mae Picklesimer. Not only did Mrs. Adams wear me out, she even read the note to the entire class. Everybody laughed, including Frankie Mae. I put my head on my desk and died.

My teacher in fourth grade was Mrs. Ernestine Ward, who was the first teacher to really encourage me to draw. (At least she didn't quarrel at me when I did.) She was probably no older than 25 or 26 and always seemed to like my little comic strip characters. I still appreciate her for appreciating them and I tell her that often as I see her from time to time, usually at the Paintsville Post Office.

Foster Frazier taught me in fifth and sixth grades. I remember little about him as far as teaching techniques were concerned, but everybody seemed to like him and he did take a bunch of us boys camping one night after he and Dorsel Sparks (who lived up Number Three and taught at the Mayo Vocational School at that time) became our scoutmasters. Unfortunately, about the only thing I can remember about that camping trip is that we went to Fishtrap, a 4-H camp which is now at the bottom of Paintsville Lake, and it rained all night long. Water came into my tent from the bottom as well as the top. I had a lousy time. About the only thing I can remember about being a Boy Scout was that one-night camping trip.

My seventh-grade teacher was Hershell Pack (no relation), and Walter Clay VanHoose taught me in the eighth grade. Had it not been for Mr. VanHoose, I seriously doubt that I'd ever have learned my multiplication tables. After a few days of my stammering, " seven times eight equals...er...er...," he'd take his paddle from his desk drawer and place it squarely in the middle of his desk. Fortunately for me, I never felt it, because it wasn't long before I could zip right up through my twelves.

• • •

"George Eliot's old granny rode a pig home yesterday."

Those of us who entered first grade at Muddy Branch in 1945 undoubtedly remember that this silly little sentence had nothing to do with George Eliot, but instead was the *secret* way we learned to spell *geography.*

That tidbit of information is among the many memories of my first learning experiences at the big yellow school that sat majestically atop the little knoll overlooking what we called the "schoolhouse bottom." The H. S. Howes Community School was an imposing structure, the second-largest

The H. S. Howes Community School sat atop a little knoll overlooking the "school house bottom."

building in Thealka, being surpassed in size only by the Northeast Coal Company's boarding house, if you don't count the coal tipple.

I have often wondered why the history books never recorded the fact that those who constructed the school chose to place it squarely on top of a sacred Indian burial ground. By kneeling in the grass at the back of the building and peeping through the little screen-covered, eighteen-inch-square hole in the building's foundation, we could see the mounds, as plain as day, silhouetted against the light from a similar opening at the front of the building.

We were warned, threatened and outright told by some of our teachers never, never, ever, never to go under the floor and disturb those resting warriors. I adamantly resisted those suggestions by some of the older boys that there were really no Indians at all, and that these stories were nothing more than mere scare tactics on the part of the teachers in an attempt to keep us from removing the screen and crawling under the floor. As far as I know, no one ever did.

When Mrs. Adams would read us the words of Hiawatha's song, "On the shores of Gitche Gumee, Of the shining Big-Sea-Water, Stood Nokomis, the old woman, Pointing with her finger westward...," I'd imagine old Hiawatha himself was lying there with his ear to the underside of the floor, smiling as he listened.

One of the things I remember about the Muddy Branch school, I'd just as soon forget. Then again, how can I ever erase the memory of the annual visits by Johnson County health nurses Lola Belle Akin and Sophia Van Horn? They carefully checked our heads for lice, made us show them our fingernails (I never knew why) and gave us smallpox shots. Thank goodness I only had to take one of those because for weeks I wore an ugly, itchy scab the size of a quarter on my left arm. The scab became a scar and I'm still wearing it.

On the days the nurses would set up shop in the auditorium, the whole building reeked of rubbing alcohol. That odor, coupled with the screams and crying of the smaller children as they were lined up and marched one-by-one to be injected with whatever vaccine was on the menu for that particular day, will be plastered on the walls of my memory forever.

• • •

When the Northeast Coal Company was in full operation, the H. S. Howes Community School, named for a Paintsville attorney who donated the land upon which the school was built in 1925, swarmed with activity. The building was used for everything from pie suppers, plays, movies and scout meetings, to a polling place on election day. The first vote I ever cast as an adult was cast in the old H.S. Howes Community School.

I can remember seeing a play called "Charley's Aunt," as presented by the P.T.A. parents with a local Free Will Baptist preacher, James Lyons, playing a policeman. Also, every Wednesday night, two men from town, probably from either the Royal or Sipp theatres, would bring a 16mm projector, hang a bed sheet on the back wall of the auditorium, and show cowboy shows. We'd never know what was on until the show started and I can remember a lot of Johnny Mack Brown movies. It cost us each a dime but Joe and I never missed a one.

The building had four large classrooms, an auditorium, and of course, the principal's office. One classroom and the rest rooms were in the basement. It was, no doubt, state-of-the-art for that day and time. About the only thing it didn't have was a lunchroom and those who didn't walk home or eat at the company store usually brought a sausage biscuit or a fried bologna sandwich for their midday meal. Those who didn't bring a bottle of pop to wash everything down, would fold a sheet of notebook paper into a cup and fill it from the one water fountain (the building also had indoor plumbing) that sat just outside Mr. Chandler's office.

All summer long, the schoolhouse bottom that the building overlooked was the site of baseball, softball and basketball games every night until dark. In the winter, we'd ride sleds from the building to the creek. When we couldn't get stopped in time, sometimes we'd ride right into the water, which brought much laughter from observers, and an end of the day's fun to the driver of the sled.

H.S. Howes died in 1924, one year before the school was constructed. There is no way the value of his donation can be measured for the coal-camp boys and girls who began their process of life-long learning on this site and went on to become everything from doctors (like Joe Spears) to politicians (like Tucker Daniel) to teachers (well, like me).

All of us who began our education at Muddy Branch in the building that bore his name owe H.S. Howes many, many thanks for the opportunities afforded and, more importantly, for the memories.

• • •

Although consolidation closed the school in the early 1960s, many memories remain of the eight years I spent walking the long wooden bridge running from the railroad tracks to the wide sidewalk that ran up the hill to the doors of that big yellow building.

With a brand-new notebook back, four or five Eagle pencils, a box of crayons and several fillers of Blue Horse notebook paper, I attacked each school year with reckless abandon. Sometimes it would take as long as two or three days before I lost interest in the "three R's" and began drawing pictures of airplanes and made-up comic strips.

One of my favorite pastimes was drawing the continuing saga of my own cowboy creation, the Masked Rider. Mrs. Ernestine Ward encouraged me with her, "Hey, that's great," or, "Wow, I love those colors," and I felt like the greatest artist in the world. Lucky for me, she didn't go to the movies every Saturday or she might have noticed that the story line of the Masked Rider was identical to the plot of the cliff-hanger serial that was running at the Royal.

As I look back, I can also appreciate the fact that not once did she ever mention the fact that White Flash, the Masked Rider's horse, had no knees and headed them off at the pass stiff-legged. (I couldn't then, nor can I now, draw horses well.)

Unfortunately, somewhere between the Santa Fe Trail and sixth grade, White Flash developed severe shin splints and the Masked Rider rode off into the sunset and was soon forgotten.

At the Muddy Branch school, the prevailing atmosphere was not one of all work and no play because every Wednesday we were treated to a diversion that seemed to delight one and all. Wednesday was the day the "singing teachers" came.

Miss Lola Preston and Miss Alice Crumb would lead, with much enthusiasm, sacred songs they had taught us over the years. Miss Crumb, a tiny, pale woman who pulled her light brown hair back into a bun, would stand and sing, while the tall, pale, red-haired Miss Preston sat to one side and strummed cross-handed on an autoharp. Once she even used a bow, like you'd use to play a fiddle, and played a song on an ordinary hand saw. I was amazed.

After several songs, the ladies, with the aid of a felt board on an easel, would take turns telling stories from the Bible. One week Miss Preston would tell us familiar tales of baby Moses in the bulrush or David and Goliath, and the next week Miss Crumb would tell us once again about the three Hebrew children who were thrown into the fiery furnace.

When the program ended each week, the older boys would make a bee-line to the front of the auditorium to help the ladies carry their paraphernalia across the long wooden bridge to their car. I couldn't wait to be a seventh grader.

The assembly programs with the singing teachers were something I really missed when I went on to high school. Sometimes, even now, when I hear one of those familiar old songs taught to us by Miss Preston and Miss Crumb, I'm ten years old again, and it's Wednesday afternoon.

• • •

I don't know what it was about Eastern Kentucky coal-camp girls, but for some reason, at least at Muddy Branch, they were nearly always the best athletes in school.

I mean, there were certain things back then that were just taken for granted. For example, just as all the boys knew that you didn't walk barefooted on a T-rail in the summertime, they also knew better than to arm wrestle with Maggie Fairchild. She could take you down with either arm and throw a baseball farther that the strongest boy in the room. She was smart, too, and won most of the Friday-afternoon spelling bees.

Maggie was the fastest runner in the room and nearly always represented our grade at the county fair. Most of the time we didn't even bother to have a run-off and the teacher just wrote down her name and sent it in to the fair board. We used to say that girl probably had more ribbons than General MacArthur, whose picture adorned the wall of the fifth-and-sixth grade classroom.

I had my first male teacher, Foster Frazier, when I was in the fifth grade, and the only student taller than he was Patsy Puckett. She was also the class bully and easily possessed the most colorful vocabulary. She could, as they say, "cuss like a sailor," and often used words and phrases that some of us had never heard before. If there was a fight at recess, nine times out of ten, she started it; ten times out of ten, she finished it.

Patsy was also the marble champion, such as it was. It wasn't as if we had a real championship or anything, but whenever we played, she usually broke everybody. In all fairness, though, I think it was because she always had a steely taw. She also had rusty knuckles and crusty knees. I can still hear her shrill voice in the far recesses of my school-yard memories yelling, "No lays, no spins, no drops."

Another thing I remember about Patsy was that I always thought she had legs like a giraffe. I don't mean they were long, though they were, I mean they were spotted. When she'd stand in front of the stove on cold mornings, her legs would get these big blue spots, like a giraffe's big brown ones. I'm sure this had absolutely nothing to do with marbles, but it's just something I remember about her.

Finally, it was a girl, too, who was the best crawdad catcher. Almost every day at recess Mary Louise Crider would go to the creek, catch the biggest old crawdad she could find and chase us younger boys with it.

"Get away from me with that thing," we'd scream as we ran right between the batter and the pitcher in an attempt to get away from her. Apparently, the fear of being beaned with a water-soaked baseball (which after only a few minutes of play had found its way several times into the creek behind home plate) paled in comparison to what we feared would've been lost had Mary Louise caught us.

• • •

In 1953 Indiana won the NCAA basketball championship. The National Invitational Tournament was won that year by Seton Hall, and the Minneapolis Lakers defeated the New York Knickerbockers to win the NBA championship.

Whether they deserved it or not, these teams apparently got all the publicity, which is undoubtedly the reason that so few people can remember the Thealka grade school's endeavors on the hardwood (or more appropriately, the hard dirt) that year.

We had no gymnasium but we had a basketball court in the schoolhouse bottom with the grass all skinned off and wooden backboards mounted on two poles at each end. We even had a real net on one of the goals. I suspect the court was not regulation size, but it was a handsome place when we got it all marked off with lime, which, of course, quickly vanished once the game began.

Our uniforms were kelly green. Or at least four of them were. My mother was a strong believer in Clorox, so my uniform was kind of a mint color—Clyde Roy Pack in pastel. Anyway, we had five sharp-looking uniforms. The substitutes didn't get one.

As slick as we looked, though, a few minor problems did occur. You see, we weren't provided with shoes, socks and other necessary items, like what you're supposed to wear under those uniforms. But we did the best we could.

Of course, we all had a pair of black ankle-top tennis shoes, but seldom did our argyle socks match anybody else's on the team.

Personally, what caused me the most concern about all this was that I generally wore boxer shorts that were at least three inches longer than my trunks. Believe me, it was difficult to play good defense when I was tucking my underdrawers back up my pant legs.

Looking back, I suppose it's fair to say that we weren't really very good basketball players. But we all had deadly crip shots. We could bounce that ball pretty good, too, and every one of the starting five could calmly sink three of ten foul shots, provided the wind wasn't blowing and the sun wasn't in our eyes.

When I was in the eighth grade, I stood well over six feet tall and was an excellent rebounder. What I mean by that is that seldom did a ball hit me in the hands that I didn't catch it. Anyway, I made the starting lineup and actually played in the first *real* basketball game I ever saw.

The score book listed the other starters as Franklin, Howard, Trimble and Daniel. I can't remember for sure who the sixth man was, but I want to think it was Ollie Perkins.

For obvious reasons, none of us made basketball a career. Ernest Ray Franklin, whose greatest asset as a grade-school basketball player was the fact that he was at least six foot one, became the fire chief at Thelma. Bruce Howard, who grew into a giant of a man, and was as broad as he was tall when he was in the eighth grade, went on to play football for Morehead State College and became Johnson Central High School's very first football coach. Big John Trimble, the only one of us with a lick of basketball ability, went into radio and became the nation's number one trucker's disc jockey at WRVA in Richmond, Virginia. Tom "Tucker" Daniel, the smallest person on our team, and one of the first kids I ever knew who wore glasses, became an executive with Kentucky/West Virginia Gas before becoming the Johnson County judge-executive. And the last I heard of Ollie Perkins, skinny as a rail and quick as a cat, he was living in Wabash, Indiana, and was doing quite well, employed by Ford Meter Box.

I mention the occupations that we each chose when we entered the world of work because I'm proud of the fact that this scrawny group of coal-camp kids amounted to something.

Our eighth-grade teacher, Walter Clay VanHoose, was also our coach. By his own admission, he didn't know much about basketball ("Boys, just try not to get hurt"), but he taught us a zone defense and a "shoot-it-you-just-might-make-it" offense.

With a grueling seven-game schedule against power houses like Jenny's Creek and Sycamore, we knew we'd have to put out 110 percent every time we hit the court.

Our won-lost record is not what I would emphasize for I've always felt it was how we played the game that really mattered.

Suffice it to say that the Thealka grade school basketball team of 1953 built a lot of character.

• • •

Dave Fraley.

Speaking of basketball, Dave Fraley, a fellow coal-camp kid who was a few years behind me in school, became a high school basketball coach, and his Pulaski County Maroons won the Kentucky High School Boy's Basketball Tournament in 1986. His achievements have not been too shabby for an old boy from Muddy Branch, especially one who was a grade-school drop-out.

It really wasn't Dave's fault he dropped out, though. The blame should fall squarely upon the shoulders of one of his classmates, Roger Burton.

Roger, who now dabbles in politics, works at a local cable company and co-hosts a cooking show on local access TV, and Dave were in the same grade at the H. S. Howes Community School. They began first grade together in 1947 and were in Mrs. Kathryn Jones' room, their seats right across the aisle from each other. They apparently were typical first graders, played well together and were good buddies. They seemed to have a lot in common, and as they settled into a new school year, everything was going just great...until "that day."

Roger Burton.

You see, although both boys were from Muddy Branch, they really hadn't known each other all that well until they started school together. After all, Roger lived in Greentown and Dave lived up Number Three. Now that's a good two miles apart, and back in 1947, to a couple of six-year-old boys that distance might as well have been multiplied by twenty.

Consequently, Dave didn't know about the problem that Roger had with his eye. He didn't know about the tumor and that Roger had to have one of his eyes removed when he was nine months old. And Dave probably didn't know there were such things as glass eyes, let alone that Roger had one.

Anyway, "that day" began like all the rest and things seemed quite normal in the classroom until Roger got into a little trouble with Mrs. Jones.

But for whatever it was that he was doing, Mrs. Jones swatted him on the shoulder with a yardstick. As she walked on by, Roger reached up and popped out his eye. Then, holding it between his thumb and forefinger, he stuck it across the aisle right up in Dave's face and whispered excitedly, "My Lordy, Dave-O, she's killed me. She's poked my eye clean out!"

According to eye witnesses, whose versions of the event vary little, Dave didn't speak. He hit the floor running. He left the room, the building and the school grounds. By the time Mrs. Jones got to the front steps, Dave had already crossed the long wooden bridge and was running as fast as he could toward his house.

"He scared me to death," Dave admitted nearly 50 years later.

He surely must have, for no amount of begging, threats or bribes could convince Dave to return to school that year.

• • •

Remember the old spelling books we had in grade school? Remember how thin they were? I can remember wondering why, if learning to spell was all that important, the books weren't bigger.

Ironically, though, of all the books we had back then, the speller was actually used more than any other and was toted back and forth from school to home nearly every day. After all, even *then* we were expected to do homework, and all our teachers expected us to take books home. Quite naturally, since we weren't dummies, we'd take home the book that was least burdensome. Our teachers would smile proudly as we'd file out of the room at the end of the day, pencil behind our ear, speller in hand.

Once outside, though, the tiny book would fit perfectly into the bib pocket of our overalls, thus enabling us to pass ball or play tracks (marbles) all the way home. That's where three or four of us would each take a marble and as we walked along, knuckle down and shoot at one another. If we hit the other player's taw, he'd have to forfeit a marble to whoever it was that hit him.

Anyway, the speller thus became my favorite textbook, but only because it helped in my deception. I'm afraid that I paid little attention to what was between its covers.

But one of my most vivid memories of those days has nothing to do with spelling. Instead, it's of one particular eighth-grade history lesson. We

Some of my grade school buddies at Muddy Branch. Left to right, Jerry Castle; Bobby Crider; Gene Crider; Bobby Pack (no relation); James Randell VanHoose; Ollie Perkins; Can't remember the next one. He might have just been visiting that day; Hobert Cecil Fitch; and Roger Ratliff.

always had history class right before lunch, and on the day in question, we were discussing Abraham Lincoln.

Fender Fairchild, who knew more about cars than anybody else in class, but was even less fond of books than most of the rest of us, and who seemed to feel the whole education process to be a total waste of time anyway, was asked by Mr. VanHoose, "Who assassinated Lincoln?"

Having no clue as to the meaning of the word *assassinated*, and probably thinking the Lincoln in question was some kid named Lincoln in one of the lower grades, he immediately went on the defensive. "Why ask me?" he replied. "Everybody picks on me. I didn't do it. I wasn't even here that day."

Well, even those of us who hadn't really been paying attention to the lesson came alive with laughter and filled the aisles with the trembling bodies of both boys and girls, completely out of control.

As you'd expect, Mr. VanHoose, being stern-jawed, saw no humor in the whole thing, and after several minutes of whacking his paddle on his desk, got our attention long enough to expel Fender for having denied harming Lincoln, before dismissing us to an early lunch.

That afternoon, shortly after we'd settled into taking turns giving our oral book reports, there was a knock on the door. When Mr. VanHoose answered it, there stood Fender and his daddy.

Mr. VanHoose stepped out into the hall, but probably thinking one of us left unattended might jump out the window, didn't close the door behind him.

A definite mistake.

You could have heard a pin drop in the room, and we could hear every word that was said in the hall.

"Why'd you send him home?" Fender's daddy asked angrily.

We heard Mr. VanHoose calmly explain, "He was being a smart aleck. I asked him who assassinated Lincoln and he denied it."

Then we heard the father say, "Son, I've told you about stuff like that. You tell the truth. If you did it, you tell this man!"

We heard nothing else. For the second time that day, we were completely wasted. Fender Fairchild came back to school the next day.

• • •

Because Miss Angie Ward was my teacher in both the first and second grades, I can't remember which grade I was in when she read us a story about a little boy who, on a special occasion, probably Christmas, wanted to get his teacher a gift. Because he didn't have any money, he took a pink bar of soap and with his Barlow knife, carved a rose for her.

His little classmates scoffed and snickered and poked fun at him as they, one by one, presented the teacher with their store-bought combs and scarves and bath powder. Reluctantly, the boy presented his pink rose to the teacher and of all the gifts she got, she made over the rose more than anything else. Because he had made it himself, she seemed to cherish it most.

For some reason, that little story made an impression on me, and later in my life was to play a big role in my quest at winning the heart of a certain fair lady.

It was Valentine's Day 1949 and I was in the fourth grade. Wendy, the lovely, blue-eyed, blond object of my affection, was in the fifth, which meant she was in another room. Not to worry, though, because every teacher had made, or otherwise secured, a big round hat box all decorated up with white tissue and red construction-paper hearts. The lid had a slit in the top for valentines to be dropped through.

Anyway, I wanted a special valentine for Wendy and, having searched through the ones Mom had bought for me at Murphy's five-and-ten in Paintsville the Saturday before, I decided that none of them was special enough. Remembering the story of the little boy and the pink rose and how it was so special be-

We even had royalty at the Muddy Branch School, at least during the fall festival.

cause he'd made it himself, that's what I decided to do. I'd make Wendy a valentine.

I was the best artist in my room, so I had little difficulty with the drawing part. I did have a good deal of trouble coming up with just the right verse, but after what seemed like hours, I penned a rhyme that would have made Shakespeare proud. I made an envelope out of Blue Horse notebook paper, carefully put Wendy's name on it, walked nonchalantly into her room at recess and dropped the valentine into the colorful box on her teacher's desk.

Following tradition, during the last hour of the school day, the teacher passed out everybody's valentines and served store-bought cookies or home-made cupcakes and Kool-Aid, and we had us a valentine party. First, though, we had to have our geography lesson. On this day, however, I just couldn't seem to get interested in how many rubber trees were in Brazil or how many tons of wheat were produced in Kansas in 1940. All I could think about was the pretty Wendy in the next room and how she'd probably want me to carry her book bag after school.

Despite her four-inch height advantage, we'd walk slowly across the long wooden bridge that ran from the school grounds to the railroad tracks, and she'd tell me how she liked my special valentine more than the others she'd gotten and how nice it was of me to make it myself, just for her. When we'd get to the tracks, she'd go one way and I'd go another, she'd say, "See ya," and I'd say, "See ya," back.

Even when geography was over and the Kool-Aid had been served and everybody's desktops were littered with valentines, I couldn't think of anything else.

As if I had suddenly developed Superman's X-ray vision, I could see right through that classroom wall. There she was admiring my artwork and poetry.

Whoever invented those old slanted school desks didn't have Kool-Aid drinking in mind, though, and I turned my cup over. It was grape and the front of my white sweatshirt was now a purplish blue, but I didn't care. I was still down with a rag mopping up the floor when the bell rang, but, strangely enough, I didn't care about that either.

I took my good ole easy time, not really worrying about it, because I knew she'd be waiting for me in the hall.

She wasn't.

I guessed that she'd decided to wait out on the steps. She wasn't there, either, but my valentine was.

She must have accidentally dropped it.

The school yard was full of kids, but Wendy was nowhere to be seen. Suddenly, my heart broke. Not only had Cupid pierced it deeply, he was now twisting the arrow. No heartbreak ever inflicted by a member of the opposite sex had before, or since, hurt so deeply.

I picked up the card and smoothed it against my purplish-blue chest. I looked at it again. There was the Masked Rider sitting proudly on White Flash in front of a blazing sunset. Beneath them were the words into which I had poured my very soul: "I'm yourn, You're mine, Won't you bee, my valentine?"

That was a long time ago, though, and I guess I got over it. They say that experience is a wonderful teacher, and I suppose that's true because I learned two things that day: when it comes to affairs of the heart, roses are better than cowboys, and never mess with an older woman.

About Me and Mine

Of course, had Wendy responded to my homemade Valentine as I had imagined she would, I might not have my Wilma Jean today.

I first met her in the fall of 1953 and married her 10 years later. That sounds like a long courtship, but it really wasn't. You see, when I entered high school at Meade Memorial that fall, she was a freshman, too, and for four years we had classes together, served on committees, talked and laughed during study hall, and had absolutely no romantic inclinations toward each other. To me she was simply this quiet, pretty, tall, blond girl in my class. To her (and by her own admission) I was nothing more than this goofy, skinny, pimply-faced boy in hers.

In May 1957, we, along with 58 others, graduated from Meade and I didn't see her again until the fall of 1961, after I had graduated from Eastern Kentucky State College and had signed a contract with the Johnson County Board of Education as an art teacher. When I went to Redd and Williams Insurance Agency to get my new car insured (at least it was new to me), Wilma was working there.

We got to talking over old times and discussing where all the people we'd known in high school had wandered off to, and one thing led to another, and in about a year, I asked her out. (Am I swift, or what?) We enjoyed each other's company

Wilma Jean and I married June 1, 1963.

so much, pretty soon I asked her out again. Then again.

We were married June 1, 1963.

Like Loretta Lynn, Wilma was born a coal miner's daughter. Her folks were Hobert (his fellow workers at the David mines called him "Tail Rope") and Almira Penix of Williamsport. They lived a couple of hundred yards from the front door of Meade Memorial School. Wilma Jean's immediate family was much smaller than mine. Where I had six siblings, she had only one: a younger brother, Ferrell, who is now a truant officer with the Polk County Schools in Lakeland, Florida.

Wilma Jean and I were reared in similar fashion, except she was raised as a United Baptist while my folks were Free Wills. As far as I can tell, there are only two basic differences in the two.

First, in the United Baptist Church all the men sit on one side and all the women on the other.

My bride, her mother (left) and Mom.

Secondly, the United Baptists sing all their songs acappella and in the same tune, and even though everybody seemed to have their own copy of the *Sweet Songster* song book, sometimes a song leader would "line" the song.

"Amazinggracehowsweetthesound," he'd sing quickly.

Then the congregation would respond, very, very slowly,

"Ahh...a...maaaay z..e...ing Graaaace, how...uh sweeet the...uh sounnnd,"

The song leader, usually one of the four or five preachers who would end up preaching before the day's service was finished, would read each line and members of the congregation would respond, while two or three would pass through the pews shaking hands.

It was quite beautiful, really, and quite emotional. But a song lasted forever.

I suppose in many ways, our marriage could be described as rather stereotypical. But due to instances of Wilma's unpredictability and sense of humor over the years, Eugene McKenzie, one of our close friends, told me once that being married to her must be like going to the circus every day. He didn't miss it by much.

When I was a kid, a popular saying between departing friends was, "See ya in the funny papers." I've said it myself hundreds of times.

Little did I know that I'd someday live to fulfill that promise, a fact that if I'd known then would have scared me to death, but now gives me a great deal of comfort.

The flat truth is, Wilma Jean and I really do see ourselves in the funny papers, and on a regular basis, too.

We'll be reading the morning paper and having our coffee and she'll say, "Be sure to read 'For Better or For Worse'," or, "Be sure to read 'Sally Forth.'" And sure enough, there we are. Those comic-book characters are doing or saying the same things that we do and say, and usually with the same results.

While our life together has been filled with far more positives than negatives, one of the latter that is still fresh in my memory is when I was diagnosed a few years back as having a disorder called sleep apnea.

As is the case with a lot of medical problems, it was discovered quite by accident. One morning when I was taking a shower, I noticed that my rib cage on both sides of my body was extremely sore and sort of a purplish color.

Not wanting to alarm Wilma Jean, I didn't mention my soreness and blueness to her, and in a week or so, I'd sort of forgotten it.

Then one morning, there it was again. This time, sorer and bluer than ever. So, I told her about it.

"Oh, I'm sorry," she said. "Did I hurt you?"

"What do you mean did you hurt me?"

"I didn't mean to. I just wanted you to turn over, so I elbowed you a little. Your snoring was driving me crazy."

"My snoring? I don't snore!"

"Yes, you snore," she said emphatically.

As adamant as she was, I still didn't believe her. I mean, no one could snore loudly enough to merit that much abuse.

So, I bravely endured the pain for a month or so. Then, finally, when she began talking about divorce, I thought I'd attempt to assuage her rankled nerves and offered to buy one of those no-snore pillows I'd heard about on TV.

"Forget the pillow," she said stubbornly. "You either call a doctor, or I call a lawyer."

"That bad, huh?"

"That bad."

"Well, okay then. If that's the way you feel, I will."

Although I knew she was kidding about the whole thing, and although my ribs hadn't really been all that purplish and sore, I did see a doctor.

So, after putting a popsicle stick down my throat and sticking a flashlight up my nose (he didn't even offer to check my sore ribs), he said, "You've got a classic case of sleep apnea. It doesn't appear serious. It can be partially corrected by surgery,"

Whoa! Back up there. Surgery? Surgery because I snore? Was he going to cut out my snorer? Before I panicked, he went on.

"But first, we'll put you on medication to see if that does you any good."

Wonderful! Give me a pill. Give me ten pills, but let's not talk about surgery.

After two or three weeks of faithfully taking my medication, I really did begin to sleep better at night. Furthermore, I even felt better during the day.

However, one morning I noticed my rib cage was extremely sore, and, as before, sort of purplish.

Once again, I nearly panicked. Had the medication failed? Was...was surgery imminent?

As we ate breakfast, I said, "Well, I guess I'd better get another appointment with Doctor Blair. My apnea's worse. Has my snoring really been that bad?"

"Snoring? You don't snore anymore."

"But I'm so sore," I said as I gently rubbed my ribs.

"Oh, I'm sorry," she said. "Did I hurt you again? I didn't mean to. You were sleeping so quietly I thought you were dead. I just elbowed you a little to make sure you were really breathing."

That's my Wilma Jean.

I doubt I could say what she has meant to my life any better than I did in a column I wrote for *The Paintsville Herald* back in 1989. I called it "Time and Promises."

Tomorrow, my wife, Wilma Jean, and I will celebrate our 26th wedding anniversary. In a way, the years have passed quickly. At other times, though, I think they might have dragged a bit for her.

Fortunately, however, she is one of those rare individuals who've been blessed by the Almighty with the patience of Job. As anyone who knows us can attest, the fact that we still live under the same roof is ample proof of that.

Despite the fact I courted her in the old red-and-white '55 Olds that Peanut Kazee sold me back when I first graduated from college, after we had set the wedding date back in '63, I, carried away with youthful enthusiasm and wishful thinking, promised her that for our 25th anniversary I'd take her to Hawaii. After all, I had only been teaching for two years and already had an annual salary of nearly four thousand dollars. As a matter of fact, I might have even promised to buy her Maui or Oahu and give it to her as a present.

But, when number 25 arrived, teachers' salaries had improved little, and despite my good intentions, our anniversary was celebrated over a salad bar in a local restaurant. Somehow, the fact that it featured diced pineapples didn't compensate.

Time had passed and she'd waited patiently, for 25 years. As I look back, though, I expect that even in '63 she knew she'd never walk the beaches of Waikiki.

Shortly after we were married, I also promised her that I'd love her forever and that by the time we'd been married for 25 years, she'd live in a fine home with a swimming pool and a maid two days a week. As I kept the first part of my promise, time passed and she waited patiently, never failing to remind me when the payment was due on the little house we bought in 1970.

By the time I promised her eternal love and a shiny new car every other year, I expect she lost very little sleep over the model and color she'd pick. As I kept half my promise, time passed and she waited patiently and asked me when was the last time I'd checked the oil in our old gray '69 Chevy.

While she waited, however, she also managed to do all those little domestic-type things that go into the making of a house into a home, not the least of which included giving birth to a son back in '65 and rearing him in a happy, love-filled environment. He's a college graduate now with a promising career as a journalist, thanks largely to her financial contributions as she worked to send him money. Meanwhile, she's still waiting patiently for me to retire from teaching so I can take her to Florida to live and love out our days in the sunshine, like I promised her I would.

Bless her heart. As time has passed and she's sat patiently waiting for me to come through, just once, with more than half a promise, her bookkeeping skills have become highly sophisticated as she's paid our bills on a teacher's salary.

So here we are after 26 years into our journey on the way to forever together and I'm still making promises and she's still waiting for me to keep them.

This time I will, though, because as I use this little column to tell her just how much she means to me, the only promise I'll make is that I'll cherish her until the twelfth of never, and that I'll keep thanking God every day for letting me be so lucky.

One thing I didn't say in the newspaper column was what a great mom she was to our only child, Todd. I hate to admit it sometimes, but to be perfectly honest, when Todd was growing up, Wilma was a much better parent than I.

Not that she loved him more or anything, it's just that she took a firmer stand on parenthood while I, in some cases, wanted to be more of a pal than a father. When it came time to discipline, for example, I'd let her do it. When one of us had to say "No," I'd let her say it.

Consequently, at times, I'm afraid, his pre-adolescent thinking often saw her as an old meanie while I was the guy wearing the white hat.

That was terribly unfair, even cowardly, of me and I hope she forgives me.

• • •

Todd graduated from Western Kentucky University in 1988 with a major in journalism. He worked for several years at the Lexington *Herald-Leader* and is now a business writer for the *Orlando Sentinel* in Orlando, Florida.

He's married to the former Marcy Lynn Rivinius, who was a copy editor at the *Herald-Leader*, and they have a daughter.

Marcy went to high school in Freeport, Illinois, and reminds me that this is the school where the legendary Adolph Rupp once coached. I guess that means she does have Kentucky ties, sort of.

• • •

The call came at exactly 2:03 p.m. on Saturday, January 15, 2000. The long-awaited arrival of our only grandchild, Alison Laura Pack, all seven pounds, thirteen ounces of her, had occurred just 23 minutes earlier.

The first of what is sure to be many telephone conversations between us consisted mostly of my muttering, "Oh my, oh my," while she, as only she could, was screaming, "Well, I'm here! Will somebody please feed me? And by the way, don't

I sure have a strong set of lungs?"

Son Todd, when he could get a word in edgewise, explained that Alison had turned out fine and that her mother, more than a little tired, was doing okay, too.

Wilma Jean wasn't home when the initial call came in, but she was treated to a similar one about three hours later.

Todd, Marcy and Alison, summer 2001.

Her conversation went a lot like mine, with the 21-inch-long gift on the other end of the line, eagerly anticipating another meal, still dominating the conversation and still telling the world, in no uncertain terms, that she had arrived. The new mamaw hung on to her every word, while Todd gave his mom a verbal description of every move the baby was making.

For the rest of the day and more than half the night, Wilma Jean and I talked about the conversations we'd had with our new granddaughter. Before we went to sleep, we came to an obvious conclusion: God is good.

• • •

It's kind of funny when upon learning that Todd is a journalist, people comment about his following in his father's footsteps.

Actually, I began writing a newspaper column long after Todd had gone into journalism. As a matter of fact, it was through his encouragement that I ever wrote anything. We'd be driving along and when I'd break into one of my back-when-I-was-a-boy-in-Muddy Branch stories that he'd heard all his life, he would say, "Ya know, Dad, you ought to write that stuff down."

So, one day I did. But, if Todd had actually followed in my footsteps, he'd have become a school teacher.

Thirty-three years in that profession gave me the opportunity to observe the many mood swings of teenagers. Therefore, one of the traits I really came to appreciate in Todd was that he was extremely focused.

For instance, a few months after he turned 14, he announced that he was going to work at WSIP, Paintsville's radio station.

"Oh really," I said. "Does Paul Fyffe know that?" (Fyffe was the owner and general manager at the station.)

"I'll tell him when I learn everything," Todd answered. "Mr. Rice is going to teach me how everything works."

David Rice was a social studies teacher at Paintsville High School and since his own high school days had been into radio on a part-time basis. At the time of Todd's decision to enter radio, David worked Sunday mornings at WSIP. So, every Sunday morning at 7 o'clock for the next five or six months, I'd drive Todd to the station.

When he felt that he'd learned enough, Wilma Jean and I took him to Charleston, West Virginia, where he tested for and earned his FCC license. The next weekend, just as he had told us six months earlier that he would, he began working at the station on a part-time basis. He ended up with a six until midnight shift on Saturday nights, nearly two years before he was old enough to drive.

The radio job lasted until he finished his freshman year at Prestonsburg Community College. He then transferred to Western to major in broadcasting. However, sometime during his sophomore year, his focus changed and he settled on newspaper journalism as a major...and a career.

• • •

I wrote the following in 1987, again for my column for *The Paintsville Herald*.

In just a few days it will be exactly 22 years since we brought home from the Paintsville Hospital, our oldest, youngest and only child, thus beginning a series of hapless adventures more worthy than those on any TV sitcom you've ever seen.

Armed with tons of unsolicited advice from every person with whom we'd come into contact for the past nine months, a stack of brand-new diapers, and an owner's manual written by Dr. Benjamin Spock, we proceeded to change our life as a happy, young and intelligent married couple into the happy, hectic and unpredictable life of a family of three.

Lyrics from an old country song say, "There'll be some changes made." There were, in more ways than one. For example, a good night's sleep came to be defined as one in which neither of us had to get up more than a half-dozen times. Thanks not only to those regular 2 a.m. feedings, but also those unscheduled alarms in the form of a sneeze or a cough, or, worst of all, just plain silence, we mastered the art of sleeping with one eye open and one foot on the floor.

It wasn't long before people, places and things that were once topics of discussion and listed as items we must see, must visit and must own, no longer existed.

Instead, new words, like *pablum*, *Gerber* and two guys named Johnson began to dominate our conversations.

After a month or so, we got to the point where we didn't take his temperature more than three times a day and somehow we got through those days of babyhood without any major catastrophes or broken bones. We did, however, have the usual number of pump knots, scrapes, scratches, scars and scares. Memories of those late-night dashes to the emergency room, although really not that frequent, are still hammered in bold relief on my brain.

One in particular that seems to stand out, and probably best exemplifies the state we were in, involves a fall in the living room one night that resulted in his hitting his forehead on the sharp corner of the coffee table. His every heartbeat pumped gushes of dark blood as I slapped a cold washcloth compress to the wound.

His mother drove and I comforted my child as best I could, answering his questions tenderly. "No, son, we're not going to the Dairy Queen." The five blocks were driven in less than two minutes, but it seemed like hours before we rushed him into the emergency room. I still held the compress firmly as I told the nurse, "It's bad. It's really bad."

"Here, let me see, " she said calmly. I couldn't bear to look as she gently lifted the washcloth from his head. I'll never forget her next words: "Where? Where's he hurt? I don't see anything. Where?"

We drove home in silence and the wounded child sat between us. His tiny Band-Aid was clearly visible in the light from the dashboard as he played with the radio dial.

Believing in the old saying, "Better safe than sorry,"

we called Dr. Turner at least three times a week. But, we always had good, sound legitimate questions like, "He ate the candles off his birthday cake. Will he be all right?" or, "He's asleep! He never naps this time of day. Do you think he's okay?"

After two or three years, Dr. Spock (or some other giver of advice) instructed us to get a dog. Every little boy needed a dog. Okay! A real boy needs a real dog, right? We got him one, named him Fleagle, and he ate his doghouse. I mean he actually ate the boards right off the sides of his doghouse and was starting on ours before we finally returned him to his original owner. A definite mistake. Take my advice and never, ever give a little boy's dog away.

As time went on, Captain Kangaroo, Mr. Rogers and Miss Marilyn on "Romper Room" kept him entertained, while "Zoom", "Sesame Street" and his mother taught him to read. Then, without warning, he abandoned us. He started in school.

I could go on, but I guess by now you get the picture. There's no teacher like experience, so I suppose it's safe to say that certainly by now, we must be considered experts in child rearing. It's a clear bet, however, that anyone who knows us very well will never ask for our advice.

• • •

For the most part, my mother was a sane, rational, clear-thinking woman. The one thing, though, that caused her to go bonkers and lose all reasoning, was the mere mention of head lice at school.

And, it didn't have to be at the Muddy Branch school, either. If she heard on the radio or read in the *Grit* that there was an outbreak of head lice in a school in rural Mississippi or northern Montana or even in Bangor, Maine, it was all the same. What resulted was that little brother Joe and I would find ourselves down on our knees with our heads in Mom's lap being gone over with a fine-toothed comb, literally.

The teeth of that comb were like a hundred little razors. And, apparently she felt her efforts were all for naught if every tooth didn't go all the way to the bone. When she'd get through, our scalps would feel like two freshly-turned new grounds.

"It isn't a sin to catch lice," she'd say, "but it is a sin to keep 'em."

"But, I...ouch...ain't...owww...got 'em!" I'd argue.

"You won't either, if I can help it," she'd answer.

I was always amazed that my finger tips were not blood stained as I'd check the extent of the damage I was sure she'd done.

As it always turned out, for all her excavations, she never once unearthed a living creature. I can remember, however, when other kids, whose moms probably hated lice as much as mine did, would come to school with their hair all slicked back with something we knew as "Blue Ointment," looking as if they'd stuck their heads in a lard bucket, and stinking like something that had been dead for a week.

And it wasn't just head lice that my mother hated. She had a regular arsenal in her medicine cabinet to combat any affliction that might ambush Joe and me. From the first frost until the spring thaw we were imprisoned...indoors. Our breath formed frost and icicles on the window panes as we watched the rest of the world ride their sleds, snowball fight and construct giant snow men in a Currier and Ives landscape.

She detested runny noses, coughs and sneezes and apparently felt that if we were not exposed to cold weather, we wouldn't fall victim to them.

One of her favorite weapons was breakfast. She firmly believed that you absolutely couldn't catch a cold if you ate a good hot breakfast. In those days before Eggos, Tang and Pop Tarts, it must have taken a real effort to prepare a hot breakfast for two growing boys every morning, but that's what she did. Although they weren't home anymore, I'm sure she had done the same thing for my older brothers and sisters because she apparently was of the philosophy that if your innards were warm, your outtards were, too. As a matter of fact, she verbalized that idea often, "Now, eat all your eggs. You don't want to catch cold." Of course, I certainly didn't mind that. Breakfast still is my favorite meal.

As we ate, Joe and I would make up little silly games behind her back, like we'd have a conversation between Cletus and Elmer, two nasty old germs searching for a place to light.

"Who're we gonna infect today, Cletus?"

"I dunno, Elmer. But I'll tell ya one thing. Ya better stay away from those Pack boys. They got hot oatmeal in 'em."

Then we'd giggle and she'd fuss at us for playing at the table.

Mom also made sure that when we left for school we were dressed warmly. Longjohns, two pairs of socks, three sweaters, a big wool toboggan and our four-buckle arctics were the uniform of the day. Since it would have taken a good half-hour to remove them and probably twice that long to put them back on, we just kept

My first grade picture. Note the layers of clothing.

them on all day long. This did, however, present somewhat of a problem because we were so bundled up that we couldn't even raise our hands when we had to go to the bathroom.

My mother was a strong believer in vitamins, too. We didn't have the Flintstone, chewable, candy-flavored kind, either. We took a regular dose of cod liver oil until someone came out with something called Hadacol (pronounced haddy-call). They both tasted just like they sound like they would.

If we ever complained of a stomachache, Mom automatically reached for that big brown bottle of castor oil.

"Here, take this. This will clean you out."

Boy, was she ever right about that.

Unless we were doubled over in pain, we never complained.

A sneeze or a cough after sundown got me a Vick's salve rubdown, accompanied with a hot towel being draped over my bare, defenseless chest. During this ritual, it was almost as if this sweet, gentle little woman turned into some kind of demon. After putting me to bed and greasing my upper body with the smelly substance, she would hold a large towel in front of the fire until it smoked. All the while, she would be looking at me...grinning.

The instant before it reached kindling temperature, she would dash over and drape the towel over my chest. Instinctively I'd take a quick breath and those vapors would penetrate my body, the mattress and the floor beneath my bed. Needless to say, I tried awfully hard not to cough or sneeze.

And then there was turpentine. I can't clean a paint brush today without remembering how turpentine tasted. Mom would nearly gag me as she'd dab it on my tonsils with her finger to cure a sore throat or use a piece of cotton to dab it on a fever blister on my lip. Turpentine was also great for cuts, bruises and stubbed toes.

Measles, mumps, and chicken pox perhaps added our names to the absentee list at school, but nothing as minor as a cold or the sniffles kept us at home.

• • •

Apparently, nearly every mother in Eastern Kentucky looked to her pantry to find cures for everything from hiccups to arthritis to head lice.

Except for old standbys like turpentine and Vick's salve, moms made do with whatever they could lay their hands on. Consequently, ordinary household items, along with a few things of nature that were readily available, dominated the list of homemade prescriptions.

Of course, that was only to be expected when one realizes that this was a time when a trip to the doctor took practically all day. Thus, limiting such visits to emergencies, like a cut that needed stitches or a broken arm, meaning that everything else had to be taken care of at the house. Some of these hand-me-down cures must have had merit, too, because those old folks who used them still swear by them; furthermore, they apparently kept many of my ancestors alive and kicking. Nowadays I wouldn't take any of these old home remedies too seriously.

For instance, the pain from a toothache can be eased by boiling bark from the south side of a red oak tree, adding a pinch of salt and holding it to the aching molar. I'm glad we now have an ample supply of dentists because as simple as it seems, what with my sense of direction and knowledge of trees, I'd be just as likely to end up with bark from the north side of a sycamore.

I've heard that boils can be prevented by eating lots of molasses, while another old-time cure boasted that a mixture of molasses and baking soda is great to rub on poison ivy.

Even the common milkweed, wild beet leaves and just plain coffee grounds are believed to have certain healing properties and supposedly can relieve a body of ugly warts, poison oak and the ordinary headache.

• • •

Even with all of Mom's cures, however, I can remember at least one instance when Joe and I did indeed go to the doctor.

It was when I was about to start first grade. I guess the Johnson County Schools required all new students to have some sort of physical because Mom took me to be examined by Dr. Paul B. Hall. And, I guess while she was at it, she thought she'd just have Joe checked, too.

So off we went to his office, which was in the Paintsville Hospital. From that day in 1945 until the hospital closed down in the 1970s, every time I passed through those doors, I was immediately saturated with the strong odor of disinfectant. If I ran into someone five or six hours later, they'd say, "You been to the hospital?"

Anyway, after Dr. Hall had listened to our hearts and looked down our throats, he handed Joe and me a little oval-like tin pan, motioned to a little door beside the examination table and told us to go in there and urinate in the pans.

When we got in there, he closed the door behind us. But we didn't know what he wanted us to do. Neither of us had ever heard the word *urinate* before, so since there was a sink in there, we each put about half a pint of tap water in the little pan and took it back out to him.

As we handed him the pans, he asked, "Where'd you boys get this?"

When we told him, he grinned and handed us two more

pans just like the one's we'd given him and said, "You boy's go in there and pee some in these pans."

We did. Or at least Joe did. I couldn't, so he peed some in mine for me. I guess that was okay, though, because Dr. Hall took them and didn't say anything else about it.

• • •

Mom was also a big believer in fresh vegetables. In the springtime when I was five or six years old, I'd tag along as she'd search through our yet-unplowed garden and along the edge of the woods, armed with an old butcher knife and a brown paper poke. "If I'm lucky," she'd say, "I might find enough for two good messes."

I don't know why the older generation referred to wild greens as a "mess," but they did, and we all knew that it meant there'd be an ample amount for everyone who ate.

If she could find "about half a mess," she'd wait until she knew there'd be no company before she'd fix them.

Anyway, as she'd walk along, she'd suddenly stop and say, "Here's some speckled dock," or "Good! Here's some cresses." She'd stoop, gouge out the plant with her knife, shake off the dirt and drop it into her sack.

It always amazed me how she could spot, and recognize instantly, those special vegetative delicacies that all looked like weeds to me.

She'd pick, and call by name, old man's bacon (a purple leaf that lay flat on the ground), and something she called lamb's tongue. (I'm not sure, since I've never seen a real lamb's tongue, but I always imagined it was called that because that's what it looked like). She'd pick sour dock, ground hog, hen pepper, crow's feet, bear paw, plantain, dandelion and poke. I wondered why poke was called poke, and if it had anything to do with the paper poke she carried.

"You're putting poke in your poke," I'd say.

She'd just sort of look up at the sky and shake her head.

How all these wild greens came to be called what they were is, no doubt, subject to much conjecture; but regardless of how they were named, I enjoyed watching Mom gather them and I enjoyed what came next.

She always made a pone of corn bread and usually fried some salt pork. She had a way with country cooking.

• • •

My mother would surely frown upon the amount of time that many young kids today are left alone.

When I went to school on those cold, winter mornings, she was at the front door making sure I had all three of my coats buttoned and all four buckles on each of my arctics snapped. When I got home in the afternoons, there she was again, making sure I was wearing the same cap I'd left home with (I lost a lot of caps in those days) and taking a minute or two to hear about some event that had taken place that day that was important to me. Joe, being a couple of grades behind me, often got home first, and even though we had an agreement that neither of us would tell on the other in such cases, she always seemed to know when I'd been in trouble with one of my teachers. Of course, had Joe not mentioned it, some other big mouth would come by the house singing, "Clyde Roy got a paddling. Clyde Roy got a paddling."

Unfortunately, in today's society, too often the mother leaves for work long before the child leaves for school and the child returns home to an empty house hours before either parent gets home from work.

Don't get me wrong. I'm not being critical of working mothers. I realize that with today's economy it's hard to make ends meet even with two incomes. I'm just wondering what Mom would think of today's world since moms have gone to work.

Another thing she would surely find distasteful is the eat-in-shifts method of serving meals. Unlike modern families who tend to eat on the run, one thing we did was eat at the table ... all at the same time, and we ate hot meals, too. Of course, since this was all before television, frozen TV dinners didn't exist, nor did frozen radio dinners, for that matter. A hot breakfast to my mom was not a Pop-Tart, and I doubt that she'd approve much of these microwave ovens, either.

Being reared in the head of an Eastern Kentucky hollow more than a half century ago may not seem too desirable by today's standards, but it did have its advantages. The family unit was one of them.

• • •

Mom had a way with words, too, especially when it came to certain things Joe and I were forbidden to do or places we weren't supposed to go.

Like when the older boys and men played poker behind the machine shop, which sat between the company store and the tipple. Just about any time during daylight hours a little penny-ante poker game was going on there.

We weren't really doing it deliberately to disobey her, or anything, but every once in a while, just out of curiosity, we'd wander back there to watch them play. Even though we learned a lot of new cuss words, I especially enjoyed watching them play for cigarettes.

"Call and raise ya two," someone would say as he tossed cigarettes onto a big red bandana that lay between the players as they hunkered or sat crosslegged in a circle. Sometimes the winning hand would pull in a whole pack of various brands.

We completely stopped watching them play one day after Joe and I were sitting at the kitchen table playing Authors (that's a card game where I first heard of Robert Louis Stevenson, Alfred Lord Tennyson and Louisa May Alcott) and, out of the blue, Joe called "Deuces wild, by God!"

Of course, Mom heard him.

"What did you say? Where'd you hear that? Didn't I tell you never to go around behind that machine shop? Clyde Roy, did you take this child where those good-for-nothing loafers were playing cards?"

That's not all she said and she backed the rest of it up with a keen willow switch she kept for just such occasions on top of the kitchen cabinet. And of course, since I was the oldest, I had the feeling that my dose was a little stronger than Joe's.

We never saw another poker game behind the machine shop, and neither of us ever told Mom that the best poker player there was our brother Ernest.

• • •

My mother was born in 1904 and grew up Julia Baldridge at White House, Kentucky, in the far eastern part of Johnson County.

Her father was Ulysses Simpson Grant Baldridge, leaving little doubt as to where the sympathies of the Baldridge family lay in the War Between the States. Mom's mom was Ellen Booth Baldridge. Family legend says that she was a descendant of Lincoln

Mom, 1972.

assassin John Wilkes Booth. That's never been proven to my satisfaction, but if it's true it may also mean that her family's sympathies may have been on the opposite side of my grandfather's during the war.

From the few photos I ever saw of her, I knew that in her younger days, Mom was quite pretty: pale, slightly freckled, with long auburn hair. I knew very little about her childhood, other than that she had several brothers and sisters and was well educated, having completed whatever schooling had been available at the time. She loved to read and loved to laugh. Her smile was broad and genuine and displayed two gold teeth on either side of her upper dentures. She must have had all her teeth pulled sometime before, or right after, I was born because I can't remember when she didn't have false teeth.

Mom was quite tiny in stature and always sickly; she suffered from migraines (she called them "sick headaches") and would have to go to bed for days at a time. She was in the Paintsville Hospital for a week to ten days at a time about every six or eight months when I was growing up. They'd dope her up with morphine and let her sleep until the headaches went away. She always lost 10 or 12 pounds during her hospital stay, the last thing in the world her bony little frame needed.

Mom and Dad actually had two families: the first child being born in 1923, four more coming two years apart, and then a seven-year gap before my appearance. In 1939 *Gone with the Wind* and *The Wizard of Oz* were the hits out of Hollywood. I had that honor at the Pack house.

Nearly three years later, Joe came along. When he was born, Mom was 40 and Dad was 42.

My oldest brother, Ulysses, obviously named after my Papaw (we pronounced it "Pal-paw") Baldridge, was 16 when I was born. Hubert is two years younger than he, and Goldia (Her name was Goldia Belle and Joe and I shortened that to Go-Belle) is two years younger than Hubert. Ernest, who died of lung cancer in 1992, came next, and then Mary Jean completed the first batch of kids.

Anyway, Joe and I grew up together. Ulysses, Hubert and Goldia had married and moved away before I reached my tenth birthday. Ernest and Mary Jean, although still living at home, no doubt thought themselves much too old to fool much with us,

Me, 1942.

except that Mary Jean did help us keep our supply of funny books updated and Ernest would often take us swimming.

Actually, I was so young when my older brothers and sisters married that as I grew up those they married seemed as close as my actual brothers and sisters. For the record, Ulysses, who married Georgene Reynolds, and Joe, who married Christy Hampton, married coal-camp kids. Hubert's wife was Vicki Williams, and Ernest married Corda Mae Ward, both of whom were town kids. Goldia married Adam Osborne and Mary Jean married Ernie Cottle. Adam and Ernie also grew up in town. After Joe and Christy divorced, he married Darla Adair, who grew up in Texas.

• • •

Mom was the big reason I went to college. None of my five older brothers and sisters had, but she insisted I go because she thought that I had a real shot at being an artist. She knew

Me, a sophomore at Meade Memorial High School.

that all through high school I had dreamed of drawing cartoons for some big-city newspaper or Walt Disney, and she really thought that someday I'd be famous. Truth be known she probably thought I'd starve to death if I didn't get a good education. I guess I was one of those people I've heard her and Dad refer to as being too "work brittle."

Although I'd never had an art lesson until I enrolled in Eastern Kentucky State College in 1957, I was always a pretty good artist, meaning I could look at something someone else had drawn and produce a reasonable facsimile of it. I wasn't as good as Mom thought I was. She was absolutely the worst critic in the world because everything I did, to her, was perfect.

So, for the lack of having a better plan, and feeling like the mule on top of the barn during the flood, just drifting along wherever the tide took him, I went to college.

I really couldn't then, nor can I now, think of a worse candidate for a college freshman. My grades in high school were okay, but I didn't know the first thing about how to study and had no social skills whatsoever.

There was no prom at Meade Memorial High School, no homecoming dances. Simply stated, dancing was forbidden at the school for whatever reason, the most prevalent theory being the school's close proximity to the Old Friendship United Baptist Church, which sat on the hill across Route 40 directly in front of the school and preached that it was a deadly sin to dance.

I had always been popular with girls during high school, but not for the usual and expected reasons. Mostly, they'd want to sit at my table in study hall, or gather around my desk between classes, because I could draw the best caricature of Elvis you've ever seen. But since Dad never owned a car and I couldn't drive, my experience with "dating" was pretty much limited to passing notes and standing in the halls of Meade Memorial High School during lunch time, leaning against a locker and

On a good day I could knock off two or three Elvises in a single study hall.

looking moon-eyed at whoever happened to be my "girlfriend" at the time.

I had several "bus dates" after basketball games, too, which meant I got on the bus first and if a girl sat down next to me, I was expected to neck with her until one of us got off the bus. Home games meant no more than a 30-minute bus ride. Rides home from away games, however, were generally quite a bit longer. The next day, the girl with whom I'd fallen madly in love the night before, and whom I had even decided to marry, would pass me in the hall without so much as a smile.

Needless to say, when I went to college, all my bus dating, note passing and locker leaning went for naught. When it came to social skills, I was a lost ball in high weeds.

Despite the fact that I was unpolished socially, and had always been too busy thinking about girls to study much, thanks to student loans and the work programs available at that time, I actually managed to stay in school and earned a bachelor's degree in four years (something I still consider a minor miracle).

As I began my senior year at Eastern in the fall of 1960, I still had no idea what I was going to do with the rest of my life. By the end of my sophomore year, I had finished every art course available and had decided on English as a second major. Since practically all my classes had been geared toward my becoming a teacher, I sort of thought that's where I'd end up.

To tell the truth, however, I didn't know whether I could, or even if I wanted to, teach. My confidence in my abilities was nil. All I know is that I'd long since figured out that my ability to draw a cartoon or likeness of Elvis didn't mean I had a snowball's chance of being a professional artist.

Anyway, for my senior year I had signed up for whatever English classes I needed to complete my major and planned to go ahead and take student teaching the last semester, then hope for a job...somewhere.

Then one day near the beginning of the semester, I came from class and found a message taped to the door of my dorm room in Keith Hall saying that Dr. Giles, the head of the art department, wanted to see me immediately.

Once again, I had an excuse to panic, which is pretty much what I did. I just knew that in reviewing my candidacy for a degree, they'd discovered I'd come up a few hours short in some requirement and wouldn't get to graduate the next spring after all.

I called over, set up an appointment, and at 2 o'clock that afternoon met with Dr. Giles. Although I'd had several classes under him and knew him well, I was scared to death. When I walked into his office he was rifling through a stack of test papers from one of his art appreciation classes and he ignored me for a second or two.

Then, without any explanation, he blurted out, "We want you to teach a class this semester."

I was stunned and not even sure I'd heard him correctly,

but he went into a little more detail and explained that Tom McHone, one of my favorite instructors, had overloaded Art 117, which was a basic drawing and design class, and they wanted me to take 20 or so of his students and teach a class of my own.

At first I acted like a pure idiot and steadfastly refused the offer. I told Dr. Giles that I had never done anything like that before and I just didn't think I could.

"You can, Clyde," he said. "I've watched you for three years. You're a natural-born teacher. You are a people person, and you've got what it takes to go into art education."

He went on to tell me that if I ran into any problems, he and Tom McHone would be there to help me, and they would pay me $10 an hour.

To make a long story short, he convinced me. I had 27 students, mostly freshmen, and at the end of the semester, my students' work was just as good, and in some cases better, than the work of Tom McHone's students.

I had been baptized and Walt Disney could just find somebody else to draw his cartoons. I was going to be an art teacher.

The next semester I did my student teaching at Fort Thomas Highlands High School under a sweet lady named Claudia Payne. I made an A in student teaching, and for the first time in eight semesters, made the Dean's List.

When I began my teaching career at Meade Memorial in the fall of 1961, there wasn't a prouder person on Earth than my mom. She never missed an opportunity to tell anybody who'd listen that I had a degree and was an art teacher. To her, teaching art was even a greater accomplishment than drawing cartoons for Walt Disney, which is exactly the same way that I felt about it.

Dad didn't say much, but he bought me three new ties at

Frails, considered by many, including Dad, to be Paintsville's finest department store.

I had been teaching only a few months when I walked into a classroom filled with bright-eyed first graders. It was time for their weekly art class and their desks had been cleared in eager anticipation of the arrival of Mr. Art. (Few could remember to call me Mr. Pack, but Mr. Art was fine with me.)

Their eagerness was no less than mine, for I couldn't wait to pull the brightly colored construction paper from my art box, hand out the glue and scissors and begin the project I'd decided was the next logical step in helping these youngsters become true creative artists.

As their regular teacher slipped from the room—she didn't need to stay any longer, for these students were used to me now, and very few of them cried anymore—I began to explain the names of simple geometric shapes. Not only were these children learning what circles, squares and triangles were, but they were going to cut out these shapes free-handed and use only the three primary colors. A red circle, blue square and yellow triangle were to be pasted to a larger black sheet.

Was I a good teacher, or what? Not only was I teaching design, but also color theory and motor-skill development. Dr. Giles would have been proud of me.

Now, in order to have time to cut and paste, my little introductory talk to the meaningful exercise needed to be very concise. Furthermore, I had to say the exact things so that not only would these kids know what to do, they'd also have a keen awareness of—yes, even an appreciation for—why they were doing it.

Three or four minutes is all I allowed myself, so after an absolutely perfect oral presentation, followed by an enthusiastic discussion on things that are round, things that are square and things that are triangular, I looked into those beautiful, freck-led faces and asked, "Now, do you have any questions?"

A little girl with pigtails and a smile worth a million dollars raised her hand.

Wow, I thought, just like it's supposed to be. They're all so interested, so involved in this lesson. Looking in the direction of this budding young artist, I said, "Yes?"

The question she asked will forever be a part of my vast store of memories as a teacher.

"Mr. Art? Won't it, if you eat glue, stick your guts together?"

You think that won't make you humble?

But I loved teaching art, giving instruction to many very tal-ented students, many of whom have since become art educa-tors themselves. I even expanded to teaching adults in night classes after I moved to the city schools in the fall of 1967. That was special. Watching all that talent, long hidden away, sud-denly emerge from the brush of someone 75 or 80 years old, like a butterfly escaping a cocoon, was very satisfying, to say the least.

But in the mid-1980s art in the public schools, at least in Eastern Kentucky, was dealt a crushing blow when someone convinced state department administrators that the Russians and Japanese were way ahead of Americans in science and math. So, in somewhat of a panic, emphasis was placed on those sub-jects and the creative arts literally starved to death. Scheduling prevented many of the brighter students from taking art, and sometimes I got the feeling that guidance counselors began using my classes as a dumping ground for students nobody else wanted. I couldn't help but feel that if a kid became a problem, his punishment was he had to take art. A good day in art class became defined as a day when no one got hurt. (Thank good-ness for blunt-nosed scissors.)

Of course, the same thing occurred in music, especially band, and what was once an 80-or 90-piece marching band at Paintsville High School (The Marching Showmen) became a group of half that number, or even less.

Anyway, I saw the handwriting on the wall rather early and that, along with my recognition that I was suffering from the cliched (but very real) "burn-out syndrome," prompted me to move into teaching English full-time in the fall of 1984. I think the move extended my teaching career by at least 10 years.

• • •

Little brother Joe finished at Eastern, too, in 1964, with a major in chemistry. He taught one year at Johnson County's Oil Springs High School before moving to Indiana and pursuing a career in industry.

Hubert, who went to Mayo Vocational School when he got out of the Navy, ended up teaching there, and probably earned enough college credits over the years to equal two or three regular college degrees.

• • •

Papaw and Mamaw Baldridge were the only grandparents that I ever knew. Dad's father died long before I was born and his mom died when I was just a baby. Mamaw Baldridge died when I was just 12 years old, but Papaw Baldridge lived well into the 1960s.

They lived at White House, Kentucky, on a little knoll in a little brown weather-beaten house on the right side of the road as you came off Hammond Hill. Muddy Branch was on the other side of the county, 12 or 15 miles away, but in the 1940s, especially since neither Papaw nor Dad owned a car, those 15 miles could just as easily have been a hundred, even a thousand.

Whenever Dad could arrange for someone to drive us, we'd go "down home to see Poppy," as Mom would put it, perhaps twice or three times a year, never for more than three hours at a time.

Papaw always looked the same. He wore bibbed overalls, a blue work shirt with the sleeves rolled up to about his elbows, and long underwear...even in the summertime. Everybody else would be burning up and he'd be sitting, as cool as a cucumber, in the shade of the front porch, smoking his ever-present pipe.

Ellen and Liss Baldridge, my grandparents, 1950.

I was fascinated with him; a fascination that went far beyond the fact that he had ducks and geese and goats and guineas and a mule that stood with his head stuck over the drawbars next to the barn. He must have had that mule for years and every time we'd go down there, it'd be standing in the same place.

Papaw wasn't really a great storyteller, at least not in the sense of, "Why, I remember back when I was a boy" storytelling. Nevertheless, when he'd talk, I'd listen.

Mostly, he'd talk about his garden, about how he'd hoed twelve rows of beans that morning before the sun got hot. He'd talk about walking down to Freddie Meade's store to get a can of Prince Albert or a five-pound bag of sugar. He'd talk about how big the blacksnake was he'd seen down by the creek last week.

He was intelligent and soft-spoken, and the twinkle in his eyes told the world that he loved the land and the people who inhabited it, that he respected the rights of others and that he had the right to expect them to respect his rights, too. He was a gentleman, and he was a gentle man.

Mamaw was not much of a conversationalist, but would stand over a hot coal stove in hundred-degree weather and can green beans that she had picked from their garden earlier in the day, she too dressed in enough clothing, at least by today's standards, to outfit half the female population of the county. More often than not, she also wore a colorful bibbed apron and a bonnet, even when she was indoors.

One has to wonder what they'd have thought of all the grumbling we do today when the weather gets hot. I doubt they ever saw an air-conditioner and would likely have wondered how such hardy, pioneer stock as themselves could have produced such a generation of weaklings.

• • •

Mom called him Willie, the name on his birth certificate. His friends called him Bill. He signed his name W. M. and business correspondence was always addressed to William Pack. He died in 1969 at age 68. He was my father.

One memory from my childhood that is still very vivid regarding Dad is the time he took Joe and me to fish in the Number One Pond.

To be perfectly honest, I'm not really sure that Joe was along. At the same time, neither can I imagine my being there without Joe. He and I nearly always did everything together. We were sort of like SamanEric in Richard Golding's *Lord of the Flies*. ClydeanJoe was like one entity in those days.

Anyway, I couldn't have been over five or six years old, which would have put Joe at two or three. Still, I remember it was summer and early in the morning because the grass was still wet with dew and Dad kept warning me not to slip and fall in. Of course, had it been in the afternoon, we couldn't have fished because this was our swimming hole and it would have been filled with screaming, splashing half-naked (and sometimes, whole-naked) coal-camp kids.

I can remember how odd it was that the pond seemed so still, like it was asleep. I can remember sitting on the grass and looking to the far end and seeing, through a lazy mist that reminded me of what the water looked like when Mom heated it in a washtub, the cattails and their upside-down reflection mirrored on the still surface. I can still see, and almost hear, the snake feeders (it was years before I knew these were called dragonflies) as they darted back and forth over the water near the edge of the bank.

Another thing I remember is that we didn't take any fishing gear. Not even a cane pole. After we got there, Dad used his pocket knife (he always carried a pocket knife that he'd never let me use: "No, Son, it's too sharp. You'll cut your fingers off.") and cut a branch about five or six feet long from a nearby bush. He then tied to it some fishing line he had in his pocket. I don't know where he'd gotten the line, unless he'd picked up some that Ernest had lying around. Ernest always fished.

Dad also produced from his pocket a little round tin box about the size of a 50-cent piece. It had a few tiny fish hooks and some little lead sinkers in it. I doubt that I'd ever used real fish hooks before. When I'd lie on my stomach on the little railroad crossing near the mouth of Society Row and fish for chub minnows through the crossties, I'd use bent straight pins for my fish hooks. Mom always had plenty of these stuck in a little red pin cushion she kept on the mantle. Bait was a little ball of light bread stuck on the end of the pin.

Dad hadn't dug any worms, either, so he walked around the bank, turned over a few rocks, picked up a couple of worms and a cricket or two, and stuck them in a Prince Albert can he'd also picked up some place. I remember how Dad seemed so tall (he was perhaps an inch shorter than six feet), so strong, so invulnerable, so smart.

What I don't remember is whether we caught anything. But if we had, it'd only have

Dad and I show off our catch from Thelma Lake, 1964.

been a sundad or two, and we'd have thrown them back.

Dad and I and fellow teacher J. D. Bond, with whom I shared a ride to school after I began teaching at Meade Memorial, took up fishing in the summer of 1964 and were regular customers at Thelma Pay Lake, which was about two miles east of Paintsville and well-stocked with catfish. We caught a pretty good mess every time we'd go and J. D. and I would give ours to Dad. He'd clean them and Mom would fry them for him.

For nearly 50 of his 69 years my dad was a coal miner. The heels of his callous-covered hands were as thick as a catcher's mitt. Once I saw him reach up to the eaves of the house and crush a wasp's nest bare-handed, and this while the wasps were crawling all over it. His back was slightly bent from working in 30-inch-high coal since boyhood and his breathing had become labored as year by year his lungs filled with rock dust.

Yet, he was strong as a bull and gentle as a lamb...and loved to grow things.

Dad had a big, fenced-in garden in the head of Slaughter Pen Hollow from which he fed his family year round. It could have modeled for a seed catalog. His lettuce, green onions and tomatoes were always picture perfect, and not even the bravest weed in the world would attempt to grow between his corn rows. Quite simply, he had a knack for knowing just when to plant, and it seemed he'd be harvesting long after everybody else's gardens were gone.

But he never took credit for the things he grew. When someone would comment on how pretty his beans looked, or his abundant yield of potatoes, he'd just shrug and say, "Yeah, the Lord has been good to us."

And not only was Dad good with vegetables, he also loved to grow flowers. Especially after he retired, when the better part of his gardening days were behind him, he took great comfort in his roses. Not surprisingly, he appeared to have had a green thumb when it came to that particular flower. In his last years he had several varieties of roses growing along the front fence next to the road, and much to his delight, they attracted a good bit of attention from passers-by.

"Yeah, the Lord has been good to us," he'd say.

I suppose the reason is obvious as to why he didn't really get into flowers until his later years. After all, he had a large family to feed and educate, and as he would have said, "You can't put bread on the table pranking with flowers."

Dad's reading was pretty much confined to the Bible, since his education had been cut short when at age 14 he was forced to become head of a family of several younger siblings. His father, Steve, died of pneumonia after a logging accident in Martin County. So just as with his vegetables, any knowledge he may have gained regarding flower growing didn't come from books and must have been the result of something he and God had worked out.

• • •

It was approaching Father's Day a few years ago, and as usual I was trying to put together an idea for my newspaper column that would say exactly the right thing, and at the same time, not be too generic.

Dad and Mom, 1963.

I fretted over it for a couple of weeks, but needn't have worried because all I had to do was go to the post office. It seems that Mary Jean, who at the time was living in Georgia and now lives in Texas, had also been thinking about Dad and mailed me "a little something," as she put it, that she'd written about him.

She wrote, "I don't know why, but it seems it takes us a lifetime to know what it is about fathers that we loved so much. I knew he loved me and that I loved him, but there are so many things that only the years have made me realize. There are so many things that I wish I could say to him now.

"First and foremost," she continued, "my dad was a Christian. He lived and practiced this to the best of his ability and he took his family to church. I'm sure there are some of his friends who still remember his charity; some sort of help he gave them.

"Secondly, he was an Eastern Kentucky coal miner. In this day of modern mechanization, that doesn't say much, and little, if anything, ever gets said about what that job entailed. I know, and so do all the other children whose fathers made their living mining coal. Few people give thought to how every day, a 1940s coal miner put his life on the line so that someone else could live a little more comfortably. As a child, I didn't understand about that danger, and I'm sure that in my wildest imagination, even now, I could never comprehend how very hard he had to work.

"I do remember, however, how he would take me by the hand and how we would walk together to Granny Puckett's to get milk and butter when our own cow was dry. I was very proud of him then."

Mary also remembered "how safe I felt because I was Bill Pack's girl, which is what people would say when I told them my name. My dad was respected in the community."

She also commented upon his death: "Dad died in 1969 and I've thought many times about what impact he left on this world. In material things, not much. But, he left five sons and two daughters who grew up to be respected citizens of their communities, who practice the same moral values that he did, and who have raised their families the same way. I'd say that is quite a legacy, and that he left this earth much richer than it would have been if he had never been here."

I think Mary nailed it.

• • •

Although I never heard him express it verbally, in his own, quiet way, I think Dad was really proud of the job he did for the Northeast Coal Company. When he talked to Mom or another miner, he spoke of his duties and accomplishments in a tone totally opposite Tennessee Ernie's pessimistic "Sixteen Tons." Dad's demeanor indicated that his crew was as good as any other crew in the mine...and he was as good as any man.

I think he was also aware of the broader picture; that the job he and his fellow workers were doing was of vital importance. The coal they scratched and clawed to the surface and loaded onto gons bound for northern steel mills was important stuff. I think he felt that our country's well-being depended on steel and the steel depended on the Northeast Coal Company.

Despite Dad's wishes to the contrary, my three older brothers became miners; one for just a little while, the other two for life. The closest I ever came to being a miner was when I was about 10 years old, and on a double-dog dare, walked about 25 or 30 feet back into an abandoned shaft near the Number One Pond. The vine-and-branch-covered entrance was high enough for me to stand, but I can remember the darkness that lay ahead and the damp odor that eked from its depth. To be perfectly honest, I much preferred the bright blue sky to the ceiling of sandstone that threatened to pop loose at any second and crush me into smithereens. Actually, I made two trips into that old shaft that day: my first and my last. I was terrified.

But of all the discussion I ever overheard, when it came to his job, not once did I ever detect fear in Dad's voice. Even when he'd mention that this section had bad top or that section had gas, there was no trace of fear. Such reports were merely statements of fact in much the same way one would report the weather. While it appears that fear was not an option for him, and even though he knew it was important work, he did indeed fear for his children.

• • •

Along with being the typical, hardworking coal miner, Dad was, for years, also the neighborhood barber. Especially in the summertime, whenever he'd corral and shear Joe and me, half the boys in the neighborhood would suddenly appear. It's like his barber tools (such as they were) were large magnets and those attracted would take turns sitting in the straight-backed, cane-bottomed chair that he'd take from the back porch and set in the shade of our two-story house in the head of Society Row.

Of course, in a 1940s coal camp, boys didn't have but two hair styles: short and needs cuttin'. Dad had a pair of those old hand clippers that he'd ordered from Montgomery Ward. They were the kind that he had to squeeze and release, squeeze and release as he'd guide them across our boney noggins. He'd turn an old shirt upside down over our shoulders and stand for two or three hours and clip away, cutting some off and pulling some out for as long as the hair lasted or the boys kept coming. To my knowledge, no one ever paid Dad for a haircut.

He was by no means an expert, but his barbering was certainly more than adequate and kept us from disgracing the family when we'd go to church.

He did this for years, until Joe and I got too old for home-made haircuts and started going into town about every month or so to a real barber. As a matter of fact, I was a sophomore in high school before I ever had a haircut that Dad didn't give me. I remember I felt like a real big shot when I walked downstairs to Rule Hayslett's barber shop—it was in a basement on Main Street in Paintsville under an old hotel—and crawled up into his big fancy chair and said, "Gimme a flat top." (Of course, a flat top was exactly what Dad had given us, except Rule left the hair long enough in front so we could put butch wax on it and comb it straight up).

While we boys never went to a barber shop when we were

My three oldest siblings. Left to right, Hubert, Goldia, and Ulysses. 1934

little, neither did the girls go to the beauty parlor. Mary Jean always gave herself home perms. I don't really remember how often she did, but when she did, everybody in the house (make that neighborhood) knew she had. I doubt that there's anything in this world that ever stunk like those home perms. No wonder it curled her hair.

I also remember that when Mary Jean would give herself one of those perms, our cousins Judy Belle (who became a real beautician in Louisa) and Gracie (they were Mom's brother Sherman Castle's girls, and for a while they lived only a few doors down from us) would help her. Most of the time Cora Lee Green, Mary Jean's good friend, would help her, too. Maybe she gave them one and they gave her one so they could pose in front of the mirror and ask that all-important question: "Which twin has the Toni?" (Toni was the brand name of the home perm and the "twin" thing refers to magazine ads where twin girls would pose that question. The idea being that one had gone to the beauty parlor and the other had had a Toni and no one could tell the difference.)

Mary Jean used to pin-curl her hair every night, too. It was always a big mystery to me why she'd give herself one of those smelly cold waves if she had to pin curl every night anyway. Maybe she just liked to primp.

• • •

Dad told me once that when he was a boy growing up in Martin County, he ate a lot of pawpaws, fruit from the tree of the same name which is of the custard-apple family. He never said whether that was by choice or out of necessity, just that he did.

I guess that's why, just like it is with me and soup beans, that when he became an adult he still loved them.

He seemed to know where every pawpaw bush was in Muddy Branch and every fall he'd gather a bushel or so and nail a two-by-four along the edge of the roof of the smokehouse, then place the pawpaws four or five deep along that two-by-four to ripen in the sun.

As they ripened, they turned dark brown, nearly black, and Joe and I hated them. As a matter of fact, we couldn't even stand to smell them. In a way, I thought they smelled like a rotten banana. As best as I can remember, Mom wouldn't eat them, either.

Of course, that was just fine with Dad because that meant more pawpaws for him. However, from time to time he would still offer us one, saying they were good for us.

We doubted it seriously, likely figuring pawpaws were in a category with pickled hogs' feet (something else that he loved dearly) and that anything that smelled that bad probably tasted worse and couldn't possibly be good for anybody.

Unfortunately, except for these few things I noticed along the way, I knew little about Dad. Oh, I knew he worked hard, that he was honest, that he was a deacon at the Thealka Free Will Baptist Church, and that he was a man of few words who loved coal mining, and of course...pickled hogs' feet and roses.

I knew, too, as did everyone else with whom he ever came

into contact in his limited travels (he never had a driver's license, but took great pride in his abilities to operate various mine machinery—he particularly liked to talk about "running a duckbill") that he was a good man and a good neighbor who minded his own business and who carried bushel after bushel of home-grown vegetables to the widows and elderly of Society Row.

The only thing I can safely say that he truly hated was gossip. "If you don't know it, don't speak it," he'd say.

In most ways, he was the typical Eastern Kentucky coal miner, and I suppose I was the typical coal miner's son. He never spoke to me, though, about his youth, most likely because I never once bothered to ask about his life before I became a part of it in 1939. I never once heard him talk about his parents or his brothers or his sisters or his boyhood friends. I've asked my older brothers and sisters about it, and apparently he never once mentioned his childhood to them, either. I've often wondered if his growing up was just so unpleasant that he never wanted to discuss it.

As a father, he never lectured his children, yet I'd have to say he was an effective disciplinarian. He taught by example; he didn't talk, he acted. He loved me enough to tan my hide when I did something wrong.

The older I get, though, the more I could kick myself for not getting him off by himself and asking, "When you were a boy, what did you want to be when you grew up?" Or, "Did you ever go fishing when you were a kid?" Or, "Did you ever fight with your brothers like I fight with Joe?" (He also had a younger brother named Joe.)

I'd love to know, too, how he met and courted Mom. Did he meet her at church? Did he ever pick wild flowers for her? Did he ever have any other girlfriends besides Mom? How long did they go together before they married?

I suppose it's just human nature to wait until it's too late to begin wondering about stuff like this. I mean, when I was a kid, I was too wrapped up in myself to care. When I became a man I married and was busy with a family of my own.

By the mid-1960s black lung, just as it had hundreds of other Appalachian miners, rendered Dad immobile, and every breath he took was a struggle that could be heard all over the house.

"I just wish I could go to church," he'd say as he sat looking over the back of the couch in his TV room, watching through the window as the "church crowd" assembled not more than a hundred yards away.

But he never commented to me on the fact that after devoting more than 20 years of his life as a deacon to that congregation that not once did any church member, except Mary Young

The last time my siblings and I were together was the day we buried our Mom in 1976. Left to right, Ulysses, Hubert, Goldia, Ernest, Mary Jean, Me and Joe.

and Lizzie Colvin, who were his neighbors, ever come by to visit, or even so much as make a phone call during the last 18 months of his life.

Mom told me once, "Your daddy's feelings are hurt because nobody from church ever comes to see about him."

I only wish that I had been more curious about the man who fathered me and my six brothers and sisters. I wish our father-son relationship had not been such that he lived in an adult world consisting of the responsibilities of work and family, while I wandered in a child-like state, probably even beyond what was reasonable and natural.

My biggest regret about my father is that I didn't have sense enough to get to know him.

• • •

Of course, those who survived to adulthood in Eastern Kentucky in the last half of the 1800s had experienced some hard living and were generally hardy souls. From what I've heard and from photos I've seen of my Grandmother Pack—reared in Martin County, Kentucky, as Mary Spears—she, too, seemed to fit that description.

All the information I have of her is second-hand, passed along from older brothers and sisters. It seems the general consensus is that she was rather

Grandmother Pack

grumpy with her grandchildren. All I know for sure is that of all the pictures I've seen of her, I never saw one in which she was smiling.

As I grew up, I'd visit her grave with Dad. She was buried next to my Uncle Steve (Dad's youngest brother who was killed in the mines) in the Thealka community cemetery on the hill behind the schoolhouse. But Dad never once talked about either of them, except to say he was going to clean off their graves on Decoration Day.

CHAPTER V

Spur Colas and Jumbo Pies

While my son Todd grew up in a peaceful neighborhood just east of the Paintsville city limits, and went all 12 grades to the city schools, sometimes I wish he could have experienced what it was like growing up when I did.

And sometimes I wish I could have grown up a few years earlier. Of course, now I'd be approaching 70 and, to tell the truth, I don't care much for these so-called Golden Years.

Listening to folks five or six years older than me reminisce about things that happened, and especially about the people these things happened to, has made me believe that those who grew up in earlier versions of the same coal camp that shaped me, seem to have developed a special camaraderie. It's almost as if the people of whom they speak were a bit larger than life; it's kind of the way I used to feel about Rocky Lane and Lash Larue.

Perhaps this closeness stemmed from the fact that every family dealt in its own way with the ever-present, but seldom-spoken-of danger that accompanied the chief occupation. Or, on the lighter side, maybe it was because that everybody had either sold, or bought, White Cloverine Brand salve, complete with a free religious art print.

Dorothy Parsons once refused to buy my last can of salve because she insisted that the picture of Jesus on the Cloverine print didn't look nearly as much like him as the one on the funeral-home fan that she used in church.

It's almost as if there's something magical about those times when a dime would buy a Spur cola and a Jumbo Pie (which was really a brand name for the famed "moon pie"), and a seven-cent root beer would last through half a feature film at the old Royal theatre.

Whatever causes the spark of excitement to ignite in the eyes of the sixty-five and older crowd when the subject of can-ning beans, pie suppers or loading coal is brought up, needs to be bottled and sold, because when these folks speak of such things, there is something in their faces akin to ecstasy.

• • •

I was kind of surprised when I heard Senator Robert Byrd of West Virginia on TV one day talking about his childhood as the son of a West Virginia coal miner. He mentioned that, as a small boy, he used to look forward to his dad's coming home from work because there was always something left for him in his daddy's dinner bucket.

Until I saw that particular campaign ad, I guess I just thought that this memory was exclusively my own and that my dad was the only dad who left some of his lunch for his kids.

I'll never forget how, when I was five or six years old, I couldn't wait to share the little raisin-filled nickel cake or the candy bar he'd left for me; well, for me and little brother Joe. For some unexplained reason, these little treats not only tasted better after having spent the day somewhere deep in the North-east Coal Company's Number Three Mine, but, even then, just the thought of Dad carrying it all the way back to us made it even more special.

It wasn't like we never had cake or candy or anything sweet otherwise. After all, I doubt very seriously that ever a day went by, especially in the summertime, that we didn't have a chilly imp or moon pie or an Old Nick candy bar from the company store. However, no such treat matched the one brought home in Daddy's dinner bucket, and even after all these years, it was kind of disappointing to discover that other kids in other places shared this same experience.

Another instance when I discovered that coal miners everywhere back then had more in common than I'd previously imagined, was when I saw an art print hanging in a Lexington, Kentucky, doctor's office. The painting featured a variety of very familiar mining paraphernalia, just like my daddy used when I was a boy. There was the typical scarred and battered hard-hull cap, a dented and dirty carbide lamp, and a pair of worn knee pads. What really caught my attention, though, was that this picture also included a half-eaten package of Tums.

I had no idea that other miners carried them, too, at least not to the extent that they would be thought of as part of their every day equipment. I guess for some reason I just thought that indigestion was an affliction that was peculiar to only my dad. Sometimes at night before he'd go to bed, he'd mix a couple of spoonfuls of baking soda in a glass of water and drink it. In a minute or so, he'd belch.

Anyway, after having to accept the fact that there were undeniable similarities between Dad and other coal miners, as well as Thealka and other mining communities, even in other states, I'm now starting to question some of those things that I was absolutely sure made us different.

For example, did anyone other than folks in Muddy Branch ever refer to the clothes that miners wore as "bank clothes" and the site where miners worked as a "coal bank?" And what about the commissary? Did other folks in other places refer to their company store as the commissary? And John L. Lewis. Am I the only son of a coal miner ever to get into big trouble for making uncomplimentary remarks about John L.'s eyebrows?

And what about soup beans? Did other folks in other coal-mining communities eat them, and love them, as much as Joe and I did? Did other kids ever mix a spoonful of prepared mustard in a plateful of soup beans and mash them with a fork before eating them? Did other kids cry for them for breakfast and eat them cold ... like Joe did?

I suppose, however, the last question should be, "What difference does it make?" In the long run, it really wasn't what we did that made us different, anyway. It was who we were. That long cast of characters from those days nearly 60 years ago still perform on a regular basis in the footlights on the stage of my memory, and it was really these folks who made my growing up unique.

• • •

I was also reminded not long ago that the similarities between those who called Muddy Branch home and those from elsewhere even went beyond what we said and did. In some cases we even looked alike.

In late 1999, my sister-in-law Corda (my brother Ernest's widow, who now lives in Indiana) sent me a copy of a picture she had found in a magazine. According to the cutline beneath it, it was of a group of eight coal miners, apparently taken during the Great Depression. They were emerging from a mine after finishing their shift, pausing near the entrance to read a message on a bulletin board.

Corda thought the miner on the extreme left looked like Dad, and wondered if I did too.

He was the only one in the picture whose face was visible. Or at least it would have been had it not been covered with coal dust. Except for a little light around his mouth, it could have been a silhouette cut from black construction paper.

But he was of the right stature and the way he stood, his knees slightly bent, his shoulders drooped, was like I'd seen Dad stand hundreds of times, especially when he was tired. He was carrying a dinner bucket like Dad used to carry, like the one Joe and I used to raid for our treat: one of those tall aluminum kind with different compartments, one on top of the other. But then again, the other three dinner buckets that could be seen in the picture were identical to the one this miner carried. They no doubt came from the company store and, likely as not, every miner who worked for that particular company had one.

Only two of the men in the picture appeared to have been wearing hard-hull hats. The other six, including the man on the left, wore those cloth caps with the stiff leather bills. I can remember Dad wearing both kinds. All the men had carbide lamps hooked to their caps.

The rest of their clothes could have been standard-issue uniforms, long denim-like coats, and bibbed overalls, tied or taped around the ankles.

The sign they read, crudely written in chalk on a smooth plank, read, "NO WORK TO-MORROW." Not only was there a hyphen between TO and MORROW, but the "N" in *NO* was printed backward. Which, I suppose, is of no special significance, except to suggest that the foreman who wrote it was poorly educated. In those days that was not uncommon.

Although the photograph was a black-and-white copy, the lushness of the hills in the background suggested it was summertime. So if the man in the picture was my father, he still had several hours of work to do before he rested. A good-size garden, a couple of hogs, and perhaps a cow needed tending before nightfall. Of course, older brothers Ulysses and Hubert would have been teenagers at that time and would have been there to help him.

If this picture had been taken at White House or Muddy Branch, the miner on the left could really have been Bill Pack. Or he could have been one of a thousand bone-weary men who, after just finishing a shift in some nameless pit somewhere in Appalachia, was frozen forever on film with an instantaneous click of a shutter—an act which was probably not even noted by any of the eight men it had captured.

All that was likely on their minds was the impact of the message on the plank: "NO WORK TO-MORROW."

• • •

Those hot, sticky days from mid-July to late August that we called "dog days" were something we really dreaded because we all knew that if we had any kind of sore on our body and went swimming, we'd get blood poisoning. And, lest we'd forget, every summer someone would bring up the story of the nameless little boy who, a long time ago, went swimming during dog days when he had just a scab from a chigger bite on his arm. With each telling the boy suffered more and more until his arm just rotted off and he finally died.

I can't imagine that I was ever without some sort of sore somewhere on my body. Since in the summertime I rarely wore shoes, most of the time I suffered some sort of foot ailment. Generally, it would be nothing more than a little cut or something, but sometimes I would take off a toenail on a big rock and would require some sort of bandage, doused liberally in turpentine (one of Mom's cure-alls) and covered by an old sock. One of the worst cuts I ever had was when I was crawling back under the floor to hide from Dad after Joe and I had been in one of our frequent spats and cut my foot on a broken pop bottle. It bled so profusely that Dad even forgot why he was after me and turned all his attention to stopping the bleeding.

I'd seldom let something like that slow me down much, though, until someone would mention that it was dog days. Then, all aquatic activities, including catching crawdads and waterdogs from the creek, would cease. Even if I had no known sores, it wasn't any fun doing anything unless a big bunch of us did, and practically everybody else I knew had some sort of sore somewhere. So, I'd join the injured souls and sit around in the shade of the old dairy barn and wait for Saturday and the double-feature matinee at the Royal theatre while we watched Milt Ratliff's old brown mule flick flies off its backside with its tail.

Dog days were simply a way of life and none of us ever doubted their validity. It was just kind of accepted, sort of like the Fourth of July; they both came around every summer. The problem was, though, that dog days hung around until school started.

We each had our own theory as to what caused dog days, and that usually led to another one of our long, intellectual discussions.

"It's bound to be caused by dogs," one of us would say.

"Oh yeah, it is. That's when all the dogs go swimming and get them old nasty fleas and ticks in the water," someone else would add.

"I know! We could tie all our dogs up. That'd stop 'em," another would say.

"They's a million dogs. We couldn't do that," someone else would argue.

The opinions would flow and the pros and cons would be debated until all of us would finally agree when someone would say, "I hate dog days."

I guess if someone had come along and told us the truth, that the term "dog days" was started in ancient Greece when the hot, dry Greek summer would begin about the time that the dog star, Sirius, rose with the sun, we wouldn't have believed their explanation.

"That's crazy," one of us would have surely said. "They ain't no such thing as a dog star. They's a big dipper and a little dipper and a North Star and a Milky Way, but I've seen every star we got and they ain't no dog star around here."

Anyway, as confusing and mysterious as it was to us all at the time, we still believed in dog days enough not to press our luck and challenge whatever force it was that caused harm to swimmers with sores. And as far as I can remember, not a one of us ever got blood poisoning.

• • •

When I was about eight or nine years old, it was common knowledge that one of the fastest ways to get from Thealka to the Paintsville Hospital was to stand on the steps of the Northeast Coal Company store and curse John L. Lewis.

Lewis was president of the United Mine Workers of America. FDR, then Harry Truman, occupied the White House. These three names were spoken around our house with a kind of reverence, possibly because the news media looked the other way rather than exploit their weaknesses and bring them to the levels of ordinary humanity.

Actually, at times, it was difficult to tell who was president of what. I really think that if miners had been the only ones who could have voted, John Llewellyn Lewis would have been president of the United States. All I know is that whenever Gabriel Heatter, in his optimistic tones, mentioned either of these three names on the evening news on the radio, a kind of hush fell over our house.

I was too young to know exactly what John L. Lewis had done to cause him to be held in such high esteem, but whatever it was, my dad sure knew. But even though he viewed John L. as a savior of sorts, he wasn't always in agreement with local union leaders who seemed to call wildcat strikes at the drop of a hat.

On one occasion when Dad came home from work just minutes after he'd left, he was very aggravated because of one such strike. From what I could piece together from hushed conversation between he and Mom, a miner had taken some moonshine back into the mine on a Friday shift, drunk it and passed out. He didn't come out for a full day and an half after his shift had ended, and leaders of the local union had called a strike because Northeast refused to pay the man overtime. Dad was so mad he threatened to write John L. a letter. I knew then just how upset he was because I never knew of him ever writing a letter to anybody.

Personally, I didn't care who he was or what he'd done, I didn't like John L. Lewis because he was responsible for my being on the receiving end of at least two severe scoldings, each capped with a slap as kind of an exclamation mark.

We received the *United Mine Workers Journal* through the mail and John L.'s face dominated its pages. With his big bushy eyebrows, sagging jowls and pugged nose, I thought he was the ugliest man I'd ever seen. On one particular occasion we were sitting around the table eating supper, and as I crumbled cornbread into a bowl of soup beans, I decided to let my feelings be known.

For no apparent reason, I blurted out, "I think John L. Lewis looks like a big ugly bulldog."

One would have thought I'd committed blasphemy. Result? Scolding and slap, number one.

A day or two later, Dad was sitting in the front porch swing talking to George Reynolds, one of our neighbors (who was also the father of Georgene Reynolds, who later married my oldest brother Ulysses). As was usually the case when two miners talked, it wasn't too long until one of them mentioned John L. Lewis. Seeing my chance for redemption, I interrupted by saying, "Yeah, and I don't think he looks a bit like a big, ugly bulldog, neither."

My version of John L. Lewis. Dad would not have approved of this drawing.

Scold! Slap!

So you see, even though John L. Lewis will likely go down in history as a great union leader, he was nothing more to me than another reason for getting into trouble.

With adulthood came a better understanding of why folks back then thought so much of him. However, with his big bushy eyebrows, sagging jowls and his pugged nose, coupled with my lifelong habit of always saying what I think, and never knowing when to leave well enough alone, I guess I'm fortunate to have gotten by as lightly as I did.

• • •

The Northeast Coal Company store was many things to many people. But to me, the large, yellow frame structure became a kind of status symbol.

It became a place where, as a barefooted, 10-year-old boy in faded (but extremely clean) overalls, I could go on those long, hot and dusty summer days to be (and act) cool. I really felt like a big shot when I got old enough to be sent after certain items instead of having to tag along with Mom or Dad when they needed a pound of nails or a box of starch.

The store's shelves were always well-stocked with food staples and dry goods, and shoes were displayed in long glass showcases that lined the wall on the right side of the store. The second floor was crammed full of everything from kitchen stoves and boxes of gas space heaters to toy wagons and bicycles. My first bicycle, a Schwinn (with Bendix brakes) came from the second floor of the Northeast Coal Company store.

When I'd walk up to the script window all by myself, my voice automatically became three octaves lower and I grew at least six inches taller. Boy! Here I am only in the fourth grade and I'll probably have to start shaving in a day or two.

Claude VanHoose, who was also our next-door neighbor, the father of Paul and Wib and two older daughters, Claudine and Charlene (whom everybody called Shod), was the man behind the tall window. Actual script, which consisted of coins of various value stamped with the company's name, had preceded me by several years, so Claude would write Dad's name on a card and slide it out to me. As I purchased a can of carbide, a loaf of bread, a sack of middlings (to be delivered later) and a chilly imp (to be eaten on the spot), they were listed on the bottom of the card. When I finished, the clerk— Gene Miller, Scotty Griffith or Alton Kennard—would slide the card into a slot in the large brown cash register, hit a few buttons, make the bell ring and record the total. The top part of the card would be dropped into my poke; the bottom part they'd keep. A percentage of Dad's paycheck at the end of the half (pay periods were for two weeks, or "half" a month) would be held out to pay for this purchase, along with dozens like it, and, of course, the rent.

On those days when Mom and Dad didn't need anything, the store's tall steps, which were shaded in the afternoons, were a neat place to sit, to observe the busy activities of the community, to watch the C and O shifter (a small steam engine) pull the loaded gons of coal from the Number Three Mine.

Grown men who worked on the night shift would sometimes gather on those long afternoons, and I'd gather with them. We'd sit and watch the cars go up and down the highway in front of Fred Sherman's house or count the loaded coal trucks that dumped into the hopper of the tipple that sat behind the store, actually about halfway between the store and the entrance to Society Row.

I'd pour a bag of salted peanuts into a bottle of RC and sit and sip while they'd chew, whittle and spit and say how the night shift was better than the day shift, but they sure were glad they weren't on the hootowl, which was the 11 p.m. to 7 a.m. shift.

As the conversation rambled from Ted Williams to Joe Louis to John L. Lewis and the pile of sweet-smelling cedar shavings were spread across the steps by gentle summer breezes, I spent those afternoons in a state of manliness, until everyone got bored and went home or until Joe would come and say that Mom wanted me.

As I look back to those days, the company store represented a place and time in my life when I straddled the shaky fence between childhood and adolescence, where just being there unaccompanied by an adult relative meant I was no longer just a kid.

• • •

The last Northeast Coal Company tipple to operate was located between the company store and the entrance to Society Row. It finally shut down in the early 1960s.

There were three sets of tracks that ran beneath the tipple. One was for gons to be loaded with large lumps of coal, another was for medium lumps and the third was for fine coal. After trucks had dumped the coal into a large concrete hopper, the coal was carried by a belt to noisy screens which sifted the various sizes and when one gon was full, they'd push it out of the way and drop another one in its place. Every afternoon, the C & O shifter would come and collect the loaded gons and pull them off to a train yard in town. We never gave a thought to where they went from there.

The empty gons were pushed up a fourth set of tracks where 15 or 20 would sit waiting for the time they'd be needed. The trackful of empties sat on a pretty good grade, with gravity being the primary power that moved them to beneath the tipple. The string of empties ran well beyond the Free Will Baptist Church and since the railroad track ran between the road and the church, men from Northeast would break the chain of cars so that worshippers could have access to the building without having to crawl under or climb between the gons.

As we coal-camp kids passed them every day going to and from school, or in the summertime on our way to the company store or the post office, the gons frequently received attention from those of us desiring to hear the short bursts of loud hissing that occurred when small hands would release air from the brakes by tugging the long L-shaped handle that stuck out from the front side of each car. But, when there was no work at the tipple for a day or two, sometimes all the air would be let out of the front car and the brakes would give way. There was a hand brake that looked like the steering wheel on a regular car that stuck up above the top of each gon, but if it hadn't been set really tight, whether the men working at the tipple were ready or not, away the gon would go.

Of course, when that happened, kids suddenly vanished. Regardless of how many were in the vicinity of the released gon, by the time it had traveled the 100 yards, or so, and banged into the car being filled beneath the tipple, no one was in sight. No one saw who had let the last of the air from the brakes, therefore no one ever got into trouble for doing it.

However, the hissing sound would not be heard for a day or two.

The string of empty gons that sat for a day or two at a time, being black, was also a perfect conduit from Society Row to the outside world, especially other coal camps. With chalk we'd pilfered from the blackboard trays at school, we'd write messages to "Whoever sees this..." Apparently, no one ever saw anything I ever wrote because I never once got any sort of answer back. Coal-camp girls were bad for announcing to the world, via chalk and a coal gon, their latest love interest. Bonnie Jean loves Tommy Ray, XOXOXO. I never once saw my name in that regard, either.

Sometimes I'd draw pictures of cowboys and comic-book characters that I'd committed to memory, like Joe Palooka and Little Lulu. There were always drawings from somewhere else on the gons that found their way to Muddy Branch, but I never saw any of my drawings again.

• • •

For some odd reason, I must have been in a big hurry to grow up. Maybe it was because I wanted to be like my older brothers, but for whatever reason, I seemed to be very conscious of doing things I considered at the time to be grown-up things. I even felt more like a man when Dad decided that I was old enough to go hunt the cow all by myself. (Cows and pigs and chickens were in great abundance in Muddy Branch).

On those late summer evenings when he would stand in front of the old dairy barn and yell, "Sook, heifer!" for 15 or 20 minutes and no cow came, he'd "let me" start hunting her...all by myself. I must have been pretty good at it, too, because as I recall, I never lost a single cow and Dad would tell me that I was a fine cow hunter.

What he probably didn't know was that, even though I was young, I was pretty smart. When I'd come to where the hollow forked in the head of Slaughter Pen Hollow (so named because the Northeast Coal Company, long before I was born, operated a slaughterhouse there), knowing full well that Old Bossy had to be in one of these hollows, I'd perform one of the little rituals that was fool-proof and would always tell me where she was. It must have saved me hours of searching over the years, and with dark coming on, that was very important. I may have been only a kid and living in the head of Boyd Branch, but I had a head on my shoulders.

What I'd do was look for one of those long-legged spiders that we called a granddaddy long legs. I'd hold him up in front of my face, making sure I had him by his shortest leg. Then, I'd say, "Granddaddy long legs, which way'd the cow go?" Then, he'd raise one of his free legs and point in the direction she'd gone. It worked every time.

As a backup on those rare occasions when I couldn't find a granddaddy long legs, I'd go to plan two, which was when I'd stand in the forks of the road, spit about a quarter's worth into the palm of my left hand and slap it sharply with the index finger of my right hand. Whichever way the spit went, so went the cow.

You think that's something, I even had a plan three. If I decided I didn't want to spit in my hand, I'd flip wet and dry. I'd hunt a little flat rock, spit on one side, rub it in good, and flip it like you would a coin. Wet she went left; dry she went right.

Dad was right: I was a fine cow hunter.

• • •

Something else that added imaginary inches to my stature and depth to my voice was when Mom would give me a dime and three letters and send me off to the post office to mail them. (Back then, a first-class stamp was only three cents.)

Airmail stamps cost twice as much, though, and you put those on letters in special envelopes with red-and-white stripes around the edges. There were a lot of airmail stamps sold because this was during the war and just about everybody had a relative in the service. It tickled me to death when Alta Lee (Alta Lee Preston is the only postmistress I can remember, although during the war someone else may have served in that capacity) would hand me a letter from Ulysses or Hubert.

I guess it says a lot about how much there was to do back in those days, but, at least in my eyes, it really was a big responsibility to go to the post office. I guess Joe was just too young because I can't remember him ever going with me. It was fun to be there when a man would throw off the mail sack from the C & O passenger train as it sped by each weekday morning. Sometimes I would get lucky and be standing close enough to the tracks so that when the skinny canvas bag landed I could grab it and carry it proudly to the post office, a great distance of some forty yards or so. I took a great deal of pride in being able to say, "I carried the mail today."

Getting the outgoing mail onto the speeding train was an interesting trick. A metal post with two hinged arms, one above the other about a yard apart, was stationed close to the track. The mail sack was positioned between the two arms in a vertical manner. The train would speed by, and as one man threw the incoming mail off, another would stick out a metal rod and snatch the bag from the apparatus. Once in a while he'd miss. When that happened, the outgoing mail would be a day late, and we'd have another bag to carry back to the post office.

We got a double-dose of excitement on those days when the train had to actually come to a stop and a man would have to hand down certain fragile items,

Alta Lee Preston raised the flag at the Thealka Post Office. That's my 83-cent sign above the window.

like a crate of baby chicks (we called them biddies) or some fruit trees. I was on hand the morning they gingerly handed down the mandolin I had ordered from Montgomery Ward. Somehow, I'd saved up for it myself, ordered it myself, and planned to teach myself to play it. I managed to learn about three or four chords and Keith Lyons, who was a pretty fair guitar player, and I would get together and play, over and over, the only two or three songs we knew. Rest assured that "The Wildwood Flower" was the first of our "major hits."

The post office itself was a tiny, perhaps twelve feet by twelve feet, frame building divided in half by a wall with a little window, thus allowing no more than half a dozen people inside at once. It had been built on the edge of the road with barely enough room to park one car in front.

I can still recall standing quietly in the tiny cubicle, listening for Alta Lee to call the name of a family member as she, one by one, went through the sack of letters.

Most of the time when we'd get mail, it would be addressed to Dad or Mom. But when I'd get something and she would call my name, it was special. I'd say "here" and step forward with my arm extended, maneuvering around two or three people who had gotten there first. I'd walk up to the tiny square window with the slot at the bottom and the bars at the top and proudly retrieve my official membership card to the Roy Rogers fan club, or the plastic ring bearing the likeness of Sgt. Preston of the Yukon and his dog King that I'd ordered off the radio.

The post office was a source of pride to me in another way, too. In the early sixties, to supplement my salary as a teacher, and since I had a little bit of art ability, I became a weekend sign painter. But the very first sign I ever painted for money, was much earlier than that, and was for the Thealka Post Office. I was about 14 or 15 years old and the sign was about two feet tall and four feet wide. Alta Lee paid me with all the change she had in her purse: eighty-three cents.

Generally speaking, my memories regarding the old Thealka Post Office are pleasant ones. But as is the case with most everything, there are certain unpleasant memories that from time to time seem to creep in, too.

For example, when I was about seven or eight, it was on a trip to the post office that I lost the first dog I ever owned. His name was Skippy and he was a little brown-and-white feist. He had tagged along one morning and was waiting for me outside. As I stepped out the post office door, Skippy, darted across the highway after a cat. He was struck by a car and killed.

I remember just standing there beside the road looking down at him. He didn't look hurt, like he was mashed or anything, but he wasn't breathing and he had a trickle of blood coming from his mouth. I don't know how long I stood there before Barlow VanHoose, a neighbor of ours, stopped his car and picked me up and took me home.

Me and my dog Skippy. Paul VanHoose is on the left. That's Joe on the ridey bob. Guess his partner fell off.

I don't remember if I ever knew who picked up Skippy and whether he was buried. For a long time, though, it wasn't much fun to go to the the post office.

• • •

As far as I was concerned, smoking was even more a sign of manhood than just about anything, including having warts or using profanity. After all, the people I looked up to more than anyone else were smokers. My daddy smoked, my brother Ernest smoked, all those suave movie stars like Cary Grant smoked. Furthermore, President Roosevelt himself smoked. I saw his picture in the *Grit* one time and he had his cigarette in a little black plastic holder. I assumed at that time that presidents smoked differently than real people. Anyway, I looked forward to the day when I'd be old enough to light one up myself.

You've heard about the impatience of youth? Well, I couldn't wait, so I took a shortcut, so to speak.

I didn't then, nor do I now, know what the stuff *really* was that we called "life-ever-lastin'" or "rabbit backer." I did know, though, that it was a weed and you could smoke it. And, with its distinctive gray, wilted-looking leaves, I knew what it looked like. I'd heard some of the older boys say that if you rolled it in a little piece of brown paper poke, it was better than a real nickel cigar.

So, on that chilly autumn afternoon when I spotted some growing on the hill in front of our house, I decided that I'd waited long enough. I stripped a double handful off the stalk, stuffed it in the pocket of my overalls and headed for the house. I grabbed a couple of kitchen matches off the top of the safe and tore a hunk off the brown paper poke that Mom had folded neatly and stored back in the hall press. Realizing my need to be absolutely alone—for after all, this was serious stuff and would require my full concentration—I headed for the toilet.

After peeping through the cracks and satisfying myself that Joe hadn't followed me and no one else had noticed, I set right to work.

With the precision of a surgeon, I rolled the weed between my palms until it was about four inches long and as round as a pencil. Then I placed it down on the seat beside me and carefully tore a piece of the poke about four inches square. I curled the paper slightly with my forefinger, placed the backer inside, then rolled it neatly, leaving about a quarter-inch edge so I could lick it good and hold it all together.

Just as I was about to wet it down with the tip of my tongue, I realized that I'd better not wet the end I was going to light, for if I did, it wouldn't.

Finished, I stuck the world's most perfect cigarette between my lips, reached for a match, swiped it across the rough interior wall of that toilet, and lit her up. As the match touched the end of the cigarette, the paper caught fire. I must have panicked, because as it did, I inhaled deeply. I sucked the flame into my mouth, literally toasting my tongue.

At the same time, my uncombed hair that always hung down on my forehead to nearly my eyes, except for the one good burr Dad gave me during the hottest part of the summer, went "Poof!"

Being the clever guy I am, I immediately dropped the perfect cigarette, right smack into a cardboard box filled with old Sears and Robuck catalogs. The box, in turn, caught fire.

I stomped out the fire in the box, bailed out of that toilet, found the water bucket in the kitchen and put out the fire in my mouth.

With the help of Daddy's barber scissors and Mary Jean's dresser-set mirror with the pink plastic handle, I managed to trim my singed bangs.

For a while I had a funny-looking haircut, but my eyebrows grew back, and I didn't try to smoke again for a day or two. Eventually, I got a whole lot better at rolling my own, and I spent many an afternoon puffing those home-made cigarettes.

• • •

Being a coal miner, he couldn't have afforded it, but even if he could have, I doubt that Dad would have given Joe and me an allowance. Although I never heard him express it verbally, I'm sure he felt that what few errands we did around the house came nowhere near requiring extra compensation. So, when Mom would mention we were not to charge any more sweets at the company store for the rest of the half, we got our pocket change and spending money the hard way...we earned it.

Even though most every family in Society Row raised its own odd-job help, and older boys always got the precious few big jobs, like mowing grass, cutting weeds or washing upstairs windows, we younger entrepreneurs still had a few tricks up our sleeves when it came to making money. For instance, Gene Miller, who ran the company store and who amazed me because he could write his name with both hands at the same time without an ounce of difference in his signature, was paying 15 cents a case for pop bottles.

With the families being so large, every household contained several pop drinkers, so Society Row was a virtual gold mine for discarded bottles.

Pepsi, Coke, Spur, Nehi, RC, 7-Up, Dr. Pepper, Grapette, Orange Crush: they were all worth money to us and it was not uncommon to be able to gather up three or four cases every week by just paying attention to where most folks put the bottles. Of course, all the kids in the neighborhood who weren't into collecting them on that particular day, just dropped them wherever they happened to be when they took the last swallow. So, the rope swing under the big sycamore between the dairy barn and Claude VanHoose's house was always good for eight or ten. The pump rock in front of Virgil Green's house would net us three or four, and a stroll along the road, checking against the fences and the ditch line, would almost always add another dozen or so.

On those rare occasions when we were shy a couple to fill a case, we checked a few back porches in the neighborhood. Some people would throw away their bottles in a most peculiar way: they put them in nice little rows next to their back doors, or even put them in pop cases.

If by some chance even a check of the neighborhood porches proved fruitless, we could always pick up a few from the back porch of the store, before we marched around and entered through the front door to sell them back. Most of the time we'd go for the cold, hard cash, but occasionally, we'd opt for merchandise: pop, candy and ice cream.

Silk Stocking Row as it looked during the summer of 2001

Now, selling scrap iron was another matter altogether. In the first place, since there was a war going on, it was mighty hard to come by. So, we didn't really bother to go hunting for it. For instance, someone would throw away a piece from an old cook stove or a bicycle rim all bent out of shape and we'd just happen to find it and carry, or drag, it home.

In the second place, nearly everybody had a scrap iron pile behind their house and every member of the family contributed to it. About every month or two, Blaine Dale, an old man from Paintsville who had a push cart and a peg leg, would come and buy it. When we had a pretty-good-size pile, sometimes he'd give us as much as 75 cents. Most of the time, though, he'd just offer us a flat 50 cents and we'd take it. After all, that was more than we got for three cases of pop bottles.

Anyway, we wheeled and dealed enough to always have a little extra show fare, (what we called our movie money) or some loose change to rattle in our pockets if we wanted to impress someone.

CHAPTER VI

The Things We Did for Fun

It will probably come as no surprise to anyone who knows me, but I've been confused all my life. It seems that as far back as I can remember, my life has been just one big mystery after another.

Take smoking, for example. As a child, I could never understand all the big deal about smoking. After I learned about life-ever-lastin,' Mom couldn't keep brown store pokes because I kept cutting them into cigarette paper. Neither Mom nor Dad ever as much as scolded me for smoking that, but when I tried a Lucky Strike that my Uncle Clyde (Clyde Bowling, after whom I was named) had left smoldering on the kitchen table, I caught the dickens.

Sometimes Dad smoked and, as I said, my uncle smoked. My Aunt Lydia Belle (she was Mom's baby sister) did, too, more so than Uncle Clyde. When they would go home, I'd count and there would be a lot more butts with lipstick on them than didn't have.

Anyway, when I was a kid, it seemed that everybody who wanted to smoke did, except me. I used to think that the day I turned 21 I'd buy a hundred packs of cigarettes and smoke every last one of them. I didn't, though, and since this was before the Surgeon General decided that smoking would kill you, sometimes I even wonder about that.

Something else that always puzzled me was when Mom and Dad would go somewhere at night (usually to church) and leave me and Joe with my sister Mary Jean. When we'd misbehave (I suspect that was most of the time), she'd threaten to put us out on the porch and lock the door.

"It's dark out there, Smarty," she'd say. "Something will get you."

She'd never say what it was that would get us, nor what it would do if it did. Looking back, I think it might have been fun to have found out.

Anyway, she'd threaten and we'd be good. It was confusing, though.

I was always curious, too, about blackberry picking. It was really hard work and I always got scratched by the briars, but I really enjoyed it. What was always so puzzling, though, was how come when a whole bunch of us would go to the head of Well Hollow or someplace to pick, I was the only one ever to get chiggers where I'd get chiggers? Once, I even got chiggers *down there* and they got infected. You think that can't be embarrassing?

When I was a kid, life was a mystery.

And church? Why were the lower panes of the Thealka Free Will Baptist Church always painted white? I could never figure it out. Was it because we on the inside weren't supposed to see what was outside? Or, was it because those on the outside weren't supposed to see what was on the inside? I sat through many sermons wondering about it and finally decided it was the latter. I decided, too, that if I was going to see what those on the outside weren't supposed to, I'd better be at church every time the doors opened. When I was small, I was an avid attender. Needless to say, I never did see anything except singing, shouting and preaching. Why on earth somebody thought those on the outside shouldn't see that, I'll never know.

• • •

On those long summer days before TV and air-conditioning, as the sun went down, we came out, in ones...and...twos...and threes...as if some imperceptible trumpet had sounded. It was as if some magical voice had called us all together, both boys and girls, proclaiming, "It's time now."

We gathered to play games, and the games we played were not bought from some variety-store shelf at the cost equivalent to what Dad might have earned for a half-day's work in the mines. We invented our own fun and the only thing our parents provided were plenty of other kids to play with. Come to think of it, I knew few kids who lived in Society Row who didn't have brothers or sisters.

As darkness slowly crept into the hills and hollows and as the younger kids began their nightly ritual of chasing after lightning bugs, someone would yell, "Let's play kick-the-can! Not it!"

A chorus of "not its" would follow until some slowpoke would be the last to yell.

This game, at least the way we played it, was a form of hide-and-go-seek. We actually threw the can instead of kicking it, and always tried to find a large Carnation cream can to use because it only had a couple of holes in one end and could be thrown farther than, say, a tomato can with its whole end out.

Anyway, the object was to have the best can flinger (usually the biggest boy in the crowd) throw the can as far as possible down the road. While whoever was "it" retrieved the can, all the others would hide. When the can was brought back and set on home base (a big X drawn in the middle of the road under the only outdoor light in our end of the the camp, which was on a pole at the edge of George Reynolds' yard), the search was on.

When a hider was found, he was counted out on the can, "One, two, three on Roger behind Claude's smokehouse."

If the one who was "it" strayed too far from the can, someone who hadn't been caught could sneak up and throw the can again. Then, all those who had been captured could run and hide again while he who was "it" retrieved the can again, sat it on the X and started all over. This would go on way up into the night, until everyone got tired or bored, or both, and went on home. I can't recall a time when everyone was caught. Fences, houses, culverts, creek banks, there must have been a blue-million places to hide. The game was never officially over, but if whoever was "it" yelled, "Alls out gets in free," he was really saying, "You can stay hidden if you want to, but I ain't huntin' ya."

The days are gone forever when my biggest worry was whether I'd cool off sufficiently before I went into the house. If I went in all hot and sweaty, Mom would surely make me take a bath before I went to bed.

I don't ever expect to see-kick-the can listed as an Olympic event, nor cream can flinging a feature on ESPN, but every once in a while, the sights and sounds and smells and faces of those laughter-filled nights in long-ago Thealka appear briefly in the fading, snowy channels of my memory.

• • •

Yet another sad commentary on my desperate search for adventure was how much I enjoyed spring floods. I know it sounds sick, but there's no way on earth I could feel a sense of tragedy and loss when I was seven or eight years old and saw my school surrounded by backwater...on a school day. If I felt anything at all, it was exhilaration.

It was great fun, and common practice, for the boys of Muddy Branch to put smooth white railroad gravels into the pouches of our home-made slingshots and shoot at the brown Clorox bottles that bobbed up and down among all the other flotsam and jetsam that the rising water brought forth. Some of the older boys would shoot at rats with their .22s, but *I* never did.

Since I can't remember ever shooting at much else, except maybe once in a while each other, I suppose it was just for such an occasion that we made those ever-present slingshots in the first place. We'd use the tongue of an old shoe for the pouch and tie it, with heavy string we'd get from feed sacks, to strips of an old red inner tube. We'd cut the forks from any small bush we could find. I guess every boy I knew at that time had a slingshot, generally one he'd made himself. Anyway, I was a pretty good shot and could really pop those Clorox bottles. Of course, some of the older boys would try to kill birds with theirs, but *I* never did.

Maybe it says something about my ignorance, or maybe it speaks of my innocence, but I honestly never thought of floods as anything other than something to be enjoyed.

As a matter of fact, as the little sticks I'd stuck in the ground to measure the rapidity of the rising water would appear to grow taller and taller as the water receded again, I'd experience a kind of low myself, perhaps a sense that another exciting time in my life was about to end.

I never gave a thought, either, to the pollution factor involved with flooding. Why, if the flood occurred when it was really warm, some of the older boys would wade in it. Of course, *I* never did.

I can remember Mrs. Adams telling us at school that we'd all get typhoid fever and die if we played in the backwater, and

In 1957 flood water surrounded the Northeast Coal Company store. The building on the right is the old boarding house.

that the health nurses were coming to vaccinate us as a preventative measure, whether we had played in the water or not. A boy named Gene told her that he wasn't taking any old shot because he hadn't drunk enough of it to hurt him anyway. I can't remember if he took the shot or not, but drinking it apparently did him no harm. I saw him a while back and he looked fine, except all his hair that hadn't turned white had fallen out.

Of course, with age comes wisdom, and now we know better. When I was a kid, though, flooding was something I viewed with the same excitement as when Mom and Dad would let me go to a pie supper.

• • •

The old dairy barn isn't there anymore, but it sat on a little slope just above the sycamore. Since we pretty well roamed the neighborhood like a band of wandering Gypsies, especially in the summertime, we had a habit of staking our claim on such properties. Thus, the barn became still another of our "secret" places where we'd meet and play.

The barn was large (probably not as large as it seemed), weather-worn and unpainted. It had been built in the far distant past (again, probably not as far distant as it seemed at the time) by the Northeast Coal Company for the express purpose of feeding and milking the cows the company owned.

Anyway, by the late 1940s, there were probably no more than three or four cows still being milked there, ours and maybe Claude VanHoose's and Milt Ratliff's.

So, eight or ten of the boys in the neighborhood sort of felt like the barn was our own personal property and the adults who still used it were doing so with our permission. Besides, in order to feed what livestock did frequent the place (besides Milt's mule, somebody would occasionally have a horse there, too), there were usually several bales of hay and piles of corn and fodder stacked in the loft. That was good, because the hay bales made an excellent fort and the corn (or at least the cobs) made great ammunition for the war games we'd sometimes play.

We'd choose up sides, fort up and have at it. There's definitely something memorable about peeping over a bale of hay and catching a corncob between the eyes.

Fortunately though, if the going got too tough, there were a couple of escape hatches handy. One was in the form of a big, perhaps four feet square, hole in the middle of the loft's floor (no doubt used at one time for throwing fodder to the cattle on ground level). The only problem was that the floor beneath was concrete and there was probably a seven-or eight-foot drop. Another option for escape was to bail out of the only unboarded upstairs window. However, the window was over the manure pile, a route that wasn't all that bad unless the manure was fresh.

Our education was enhanced a good deal, too, in that old barn loft, especially if any of the older boys happened to be among our number. I can remember us all laughing heartily at the Liza and Rastus stories. However, I was probably the only one there who didn't understand them or know why they were supposed to be funny. About the only profanity we younger boys used was an occasional "God-dog it," or at least a version of it, as in, "You God-dogged old hateful devil, I'll bust your head with a rock." Although the older boys taught us how to do some serious cussin', we seldom did.

• • •

Upcoming special events were often advertised by people in cars with large, bell-shaped loudspeakers on top of them driving slowly through the neighborhood. Chased by barking dogs and kids on bicycles, the giant speakers on wheels would often trumpet the fiddle and banjos of a bluegrass band, interrupted intermittently with announcements of what was showing at the Cain Auto or Prestonsburg Drive-In theatres. Everybody who wasn't completely deaf knew that Dusty Rivers and the Rangers, local stars at Paintsville's new radio station WSIP, would be playing at the Muddy Branch school house "this coming Friday night at the big pie supper."

Once in a while, the message of some big politician running for jailer or high sheriff would echo between the hills and hollows as these noisy intrusions shattered the silence of the otherwise peaceful existence.

Regardless of the news being delivered, these commercials on wheels usually attracted a good deal of attention. Such was the case on one particular afternoon when the boys' game of marbles and the girls' preoccupation with hopscotch were intruded upon with the proclamation that free funny books would be given away. All we had to do was follow the car until it parked at the mouth of the hollow.

Wow! Free funny books?

Since almost everybody I knew read and traded funny books, as far as we were concerned, this announcement could have come straight from Heaven.

Well, not quite. The books were of a religious nature, though. As a matter of fact, they were based on stories from the Bible. So, quite naturally, we called them "Jesus funny books." The two men giving them away represented some strange church "from away from here." I say strange in that they weren't Free Will Baptists.

There must have been at least two dozen kids surrounding the car as one man continued to announce over the loud speakers to "come one, come all and get your free funny books," while a tall, skinny, pale young man wearing wire-rimmed glasses and a tie, passed out the free Jesus funny books, all exactly alike, from the brown pasteboard box he'd set on the hood of the car.

We all eagerly grabbed our copy, took it home, and read it. I didn't enjoy it very much, though, because I already knew about David and Goliath and about Jesus walking on the water. Besides, half the fun of reading funny books back in those days was trading them to someone else after you'd read them. Since everybody else had gotten a copy of the same book I had, with whom was I to trade?

• • •

Joe and I really looked forward to those times when Hubert, who had gotten a job working in the mines at Jenkins when he first came back from the Navy, would come home on weekends and take us to the newsstand in town and buy each of us ten new funny books.

Sometimes, it'd take 30 or 40 minutes of browsing before we'd find the ten we wanted. Hubert, who apparently realized that this was very important stuff, would wait patiently, then pay the man two dollars, and Joe and I would be set for many hours of enjoyable reading.

Joe would generally pick out books like *Casper*, *Donald Duck* and *Little Lulu*, and I'd pretty much stick to westerns, like *Kid Colt*, *Gene Autry* and *Tom Mix*.

That's me on the right, reading a funny book. Next to me is Patsy Grace Reynolds, who lived next door. Joe is on the left. The girl holding the baby must have been someone visiting Patsy. I've no idea who she is.

After Mary Jean got out of high school and started working at the fountain, which connected to the lobby of the Royal theatre but which could also be entered directly from Second Street, she too started bringing us new funny books on a regular basis.

But regardless of who gave them to us or their titles, one thing that every last one of those funny books had in common was the big full-page ad inside the back cover urging me to enroll in the Charles Atlas body-building course.

I'd be a rich man today if I had a dollar for every time I saw that picture of Charles Atlas flexing his muscles and posing in his leopard-skin trunks. I could recite from memory the dialogue in the little cartoon strip about the big guy with muscles who kicked sand into the face of the little puny guy with the caved-in chest (like mine) and the pretty girlfriend.

The little puny guy with the caved-in chest would then discover the Charles Atlas ad and mail in his coupon. Then, in the last frame, he'd still have the little puny guy's head, but he'd have a body just like the first guy with all the muscles, except better.

Then, he'd mash the big guy's mouth and say, "Take that, you bully!"

All the while, I'd wonder if it would be worth the effort on my part to try to raise enough money to pay for that course and enroll in it myself. I can't remember what it would have cost me, but I can remember thinking that I'd have to gather up a right smart bit of pop bottles before I could ever come up with that much. And if I could have, by some miracle, gotten my hands on that much cash, I'd probably have ended up spending it on more funny books.

Anyway, I guess that anyone who knows me now knows I never mailed that coupon. Thankfully, a prerequisite for getting Wilma Jean didn't require my enrolling in Bodybuilding 101. I also guess I just figured that the little puny guy with the caved-in chest already had the pretty girlfriend and if he'd taken her to a good double-feature movie instead of the beach, he wouldn't have had sand kicked on him in the first place. Then, he wouldn't have had to waste all his money building muscles that didn't match his head.

• • •

With our pockets full of marble-size railroad gravels and our home-made slingshots, a bunch of us once decided to rid the world of rats, so we headed to the old dairy barn and sat for nearly an hour before one came into view under the corn crib in the stall where Milt Ratliff kept an old, half-blind mule.

All four of us shot at the same time and one of us accidentally shot the mule in the rump. He cut a real shine and even kicked some of the boards off one side of the stall. We saw, of course, that the animal was really more startled than harmed and thought the whole thing was quite funny. As a matter of fact, I was about to accidentally shoot him again when Milt, having been close by and no doubt hearing the racket the mule had made, suddenly appeared. He angrily threatened to call the law on us if we didn't put away our weapons and go to the house.

Of course, he being an adult and we being mere 10-year-olds, we did just that...at least until he'd calmed the mule and left the scene.

An hour or two later, however, a strange car (strange here meaning that none of us knew to whom it belonged) pulled into the neighborhood and a man got out, wearing a white shirt with the sleeves rolled up and a tie.

As we watched from a safe distance, he walked onto Claude VanHoose's porch and began knocking on the door.

That's when one of us said quietly, "Milt's called the law and they're looking for us."

Instantly, we scattered in every direction. Some of us headed over the creek bank, others went home and I ran into our yard and crawled under our floor, as far back as I could get.

I don't know how long I stayed under there, but when I finally crawfished out, I found that everybody else had gathered beneath the huge sycamore. Libby Ann Green was shuffling a stack of cards that the man in the strange car had paid her a quarter to hand out door-to-door. The cards read, "Vote for Charles O. 'Buzzy' Wheeler for County Court Clerk."

• • •

Sometimes it amazes me when I get to thinking about some of the other things we used to do for fun.

I mean, I'm not a cruel person by nature and I'd never catch a butterfly and pull off its wings just for meanness. Neither would I beat a dog or anything like that. As a matter of fact, I'd even get upset when some of those old mean boys would catch a stray dog that had the misfortune to wander into the neighborhood and tie a Carnation cream can filled with pea-size railroad gravels to its tail. The faster the dog would run to escape the clattering, the more the can would clatter. The more the can clattered, the more those boys would laugh and the madder I'd get.

Being obviously more humane, though, didn't necessarily make me braver. I never had the courage to match my convictions and never said anything because I didn't want one of them to imitate Joe Louis and mash my mouth. And besides, their shenanigans served a good purpose because stray dogs didn't stay strayed when they'd stray into Society Row.

Anyway, I've always considered myself a civil and decent sort, yet, when I think back to some of the things we kids would do, I really begin to wonder.

Take what I'd do to the June bug, for example. I'd never give a second thought to catching one (they were easy to catch), tying a long piece of string around one of its back legs and making it fly in circles 'round and 'round my head until I'd become tired or it'd break off its leg and fly away.

And the poor lightning bug. When the sun went down and

darkness settled in, bringing with it a thousand songs from unseen, nameless insects, I'd catch Mr. Lightning Bug and break him slap in two just as he'd blink. Then I'd decorate my fingers and wrists with smelly phosphorescent rings and bracelets. The lightning bug and I were both delighted.

Once I even got the bright idea that if I caught a bunch of lightning bugs and put them into a big-mouthed Mason jar and set them by my bed at night, the odds were pretty good that eventually, just one time, they'd all blink at the exact instant and light up my whole room.

I chased around in the front yard for more than an hour and must have had a hundred of them in a jar. I'm sure my idea was a good one, but, I fell asleep before they could get synchronized, and even though I'd punched holes in the lid so they could breathe, all the lightning bugs died in the jar before I remembered late the next day to turn them loose.

And, as I recall, none of us would hesitate to mercilessly impale live grasshoppers and fish worms onto bent straight pins to dangle in front of chub minnows beneath the railroad crossing at the mouth of Society Row.

Furthermore, we were sometimes less than kind to certain classes of *Homo Sapiens,* namely, any kid who was younger than the rest of us.

Now, don't misunderstand. We wouldn't attack them with instruments of torture or anything like that; it was sort of like we'd play with their minds a little bit. For example, in the summertime we ran the hills of Thealka ragged playing war and cowboys. Invariably, we'd find ourselves all the way back on top of one of the highest ridges, out of sight, and sometimes sound (well, you could always hear the tipple running and car horns and stuff). And more often than not, there'd be some little fellow with us who was actually too tiny to be that far back in the woods. Suddenly, one of the older boys would say, "I guess it's been long enough, don't you?" Right on cue, just as if it were rehearsed, and it more or less was since we did it at every opportunity, another boy would say, "Yeah, I guess it has. Whatcha gonna do with your share of the money, anyway?"

"I'm going to the show ten times and buy 20 big Spur colas. What about you?"

"I'm going to use mine to go to the carnival when I go to the Fourth of July."

We'd keep talking like that until curiosity got the best of the little fellow and he'd finally ask, "What you all talking about? What money?"

Then one of us would say, "We're figuring out how to spend the money your mommy gave us to keep you back here in these hills long enough for all them to have time to pack and move and run away and leave you."

I could never figure out why, but when those little boys would tear off that hill, they'd never stick to the path. It was almost as if it was a law that they hit every thicket and briar patch on the hill.

Anyway, those of us who grew up in a pre-TV Eastern Kentucky coal camp found fun and entertainment in a variety of places. Thinking about it, though, makes me realize that it's a thousand wonders that we were not all warped and that any of us turned out as well as we did.

Even though I suspect it's merely my way of soothing my conscience a bit, for all the good it does, I do freely admit that I am embarrassed and even somewhat ashamed about some of the things we did. And, I defy anyone to give a logical answer for our actions. The scary part is, at the time we did them, they seemed like the natural thing to do.

For example, I'd have been all over son Todd had I discovered that he'd treated anybody like we did an old man we all knew simply as Ray Jake. He appeared to be about 50 years old, was always dirty looking and always wore what once had been a red, leather cap with ear flaps, always flapping. Now, he didn't live in Muddy Branch (at least not in our part) but, for whatever reason, visited there often and we all knew him by sight. After he had passed, we'd all drop whatever we were doing and haul off and crow like a rooster at the top of our lungs. I'm sure we looked like we were possessed, or something, as six or eight of us stood with our heads thrown back, flapping our elbows against our ribs, giving our very best imitation of old chanticleer.

But it always produced the desired effect, which was to infuriate him to the point where he'd pick up a rock or a piece of coal the size of his fist and try to decapitate one of us with it. He'd cuss and throw and call us "damn little iddits," until we'd either take shelter behind a coal gon or put enough distance between us to be out of range. He'd yell, "I'm gonna tell your daddy, I'm gonna tell your daddy! You're all damn little iddits."

I can't remember any of his rocks ever hitting anybody, or even coming close, for that matter, but as I look back now, I think it might have taught us a good lesson if one of his missiles had found its mark. I've no idea why this particular old man was targeted as the recipient of our taunting, but if Dad had ever caught me tormenting him, I'd have ended up in big trouble. I guess it was a risk I was willing to take...just for the sake of fun.

It's rather ironic, but Ray Jake also got Dad into a little trouble, too, with Mom. Every once in a while, especially in the wintertime, as he would pass through the neighborhood, Ray Jake would come to our house to bum a meal, and once in a while he'd ask if he could stay all night. One time, on a particularly cold night, Dad let him. Of course, we had no extra bed, so he slept on a pallet that Mom put on the floor in front of the fire.

The next morning, after he'd eaten one of Mom's hearty breakfasts and gone his merry way, words like *dirty* and *smelly* dominated Mom's tirade, which she underlined by burning the quilts on which the old man had slept.

Dad sat in a straight-backed, cane-bottomed chair, stared at the fire and never said a word. His benevolence may have been appreciated by his now-departed guest, but it certainly wasn't appreciated by Mom.

I don't know what became of Ray Jake. As I grew older and became interested in other things, his visits to the neighborhood became less and less frequent and I guess I sort of forgot about him. I hope he forgot about me, too.

• • •

The Ray Jake incident was just one example of how his good heartedness got Dad into trouble. Another act of kindness gone awry occurred when he and fellow-deacon Johnny Castle were put in charge of distributing baskets of food to the needy families in the community at Christmas time.

Apparently, without asking anyone except God, they toted several boxes of canned goods to a young widow with several small children.

The fact that at least two of the children were born several years after her husband had died didn't bother Dad and Johnny, but it did irritate a few of the holier-than-thou wives of several of their fellow brethren, who demanded they resign their posts. It apparently prompted some discussion in a specially called meeting.

"What'd you tell them, Willie?" Mom asked.

"I told them those kids hadn't done anything wrong and they were the ones that was hungry," he answered.

"Good," she said.

That's the last I ever heard of the incident.

• • •

I can still remember quite clearly the names and faces of fellow ten-year-old rogues who, usually on Halloween, but not exclusively then, would entertain ourselves on crisp, moon-filled autumn nights (never in the summertime because it was too hot) by hiding or switching the furniture on the front porches of the houses in Silk Stocking Row. Sometimes we'd roam the neighborhood until as late as nine o'clock.

However, all such thievery in Society Row back in those days was really all in fun, and to my knowledge, no one ever really lost anything.

You see, we didn't steal, we only borrowed. And what we borrowed was of little or no value and couldn't have been sold, anyway. All anybody had in the way of porch furniture was maybe a few straight-backed, cane-bottomed chairs and a wooden swing.

Anyway, it wasn't uncommon for a neighbor to yell to Dad, "Hey, Bill? This your chair? Don't know where mine is."

"Yeah, that's mine," Dad would say. "I think I saw yours on the top of the smoke house."

Our parents didn't seem to care if their chairs were switched or disappeared for a day or two. They'd just switch them back and wait for the pranksters to strike again, probably thinking that there were worse things that their kids could be doing. Instead of getting upset, they were probably relieved.

Among those "worst things" was something we saved ex-clusively for those neighbors with whom we kids could not get along...like the ones who wouldn't let us in their yards to retrieve our baseball or who were constantly yelling at us for making too much noise, and stuff like that.

What we'd do is wait until after dark and get us a brown paper poke and scoop up a pile of fresh cow manure, which was always readily available in and around the old dairy barn. We'd shovel it into the poke, sneak up to the victim's porch, set the poke afire and drop it on the porch. Then, we'd knock on the door, yell "Fire!" and run. When the neighbor came run-ning out onto the porch, he'd see the little fire and stomp it out. You can figure out the rest. Sometimes we'd use fresh dog-doo if we could find any.

Halloween "trick or treat" as it exists today was unheard of then. The reason, I suppose, is that we were more interested in trick than in treat. Not that we didn't love candy and sweets, but it was very unlikely that the neighbors had any to hand out.

The night before Halloween was designated as "corn night." We would simply wait until dark, then walk between rows of houses and pepper them with shelled corn, no doubt striking terror into the hearts of the occupants. When we ran out of corn, which generally didn't take long because shelling corn was work, we'd take a big bar of lye soap and soap every win-dow we could reach.

Another tale that nearly always surfaced about this time pertained to a grown man who got carried away with Hallow-een and as a prank chopped down a large tree and blocked the highway traffic. Late that night his own little boy got sick and before the man could unblock the road and get the child to the hospital, the child died. (He was probably related to the name-less little boy whose arm rotted off when he went swimming during dog days and had a chigger bite on his arm.)

Although the man and boy were never identified, all the kids in the neighborhood believed that story. More than fifty years later, I'm still not sure whether it was true.

Even though swapping chairs, doo-dropping and road-blocking were primarily male sports, and although we'd never heard of the word *chauvinistic*, we weren't. Sometimes we'd purposefully play less-adventuresome games just so the girls could play.

Take potato roasting, for instance. It wasn't really a game, I suppose, but was lots of fun nevertheless. Especially on those evenings when it was chilly enough to see your breath and we'd need a sweater or jacket, we'd gather up firewood from wherever we could find it (crossties were excellent because they'd been creosoted) and build a big bonfire. As the heat would carry large bright-orange sparks high into the night sky, we'd drop the potatoes in (remember, this was before aluminum foil) and roast them.

Sometimes the potatoes would burn so black and so deep that we couldn't eat them, but when we'd pull them out in time and let them cool enough so we could peel away the burnt crust, they were delicious.

• • •

Baseball was strictly for boys, and I played with all the zeal that a coal miner's kid could muster.

When we'd skin the grass off the infield and really take the time to pick up the rocks, and when we could find enough scrap lumber and discarded chicken wire to build a backstop, we really had a dandy ball diamond in the schoolhouse bottom. To be sure, it was no Yankee Stadium, but it was more than sufficient for the rag-tag bunch we were. We'd gather after supper on those long summer evenings, without uniforms, without coaches, without umpires, and most important, without some parent calling us names because we let a grounder skip between our legs.

We'd choose up sides, flip wet and dry for bats and sometimes we'd even have seven or eight, or even ten to twelve, on a side. Occasionally, we'd have four or five real baseball gloves, too, that we'd take turns using. Of course, the first baseman always had one. So did the "hind catcher."

Seldom, though, did we play with a new baseball. If someone did happen to buy one, we'd only pass with it until it got real dirty. Only then would it be thrown out to be hit.

It was almost impossible for us to wear out a baseball. We could lose it easily enough, however, especially if it were hit to deep left field, since no one ever bothered to mow the chest-high horse weeds that grew there.

If the ball got wet in the creek that in some places ran swift and deep no more than 15 feet behind home plate, one of us would take it home at the end of the day and bake it in the oven. If the cover came off, we'd take a roll of that black tape that miners alway had in vast quantities around the house, and we'd tape it really good. It wasn't by any means as good as new, but a black baseball was better than no baseball.

While I was very much aware of the exploits of big leaguers like Jackie Robinson, Ted Williams and Ewell Blackwell, I sometimes think that I imagined myself playing in the shadows of legends from Muddy Branch, too. Many's the time I heard some of the older men who'd stand around and watch us play compare us to folks like Russell Spears, Ora Curnutte, Scott Castle or Theodore Miller. Although I was too young to have seen any of them play, I'd heard their names mentioned so often that I knew that any comparison of my skills to theirs was an extreme compliment.

Furthermore, I'd be a rich man today if I had a dollar for every time I heard about the ball Pick Colvin hit that landed in the top of the big sycamore that stood behind the school house. I really wish I had seen that because the school building itself stood on top of a little knoll a good 400 feet from home plate.

I don't suppose they could be considered legends, but my generation had its share of good players, too. I have personally witnessed Cracker Bill Castle abruptly end the game by driving our only ball so far up the hollow to the right of the school house that it couldn't be found. Most of the time we didn't even bother to go look for it. Somebody would say, "Let's go to the house," and we would.

I witnessed, too, the slick fielding of Tucker Daniel and the pea-size fast ball of Bobby Lyons. Also, Roger Ratliff, when he could get hold of a relatively new ball, could throw a curve you wouldn't believe.

All that, though, was a long time ago. It was a time when baseball cards came in Red Man chewing tobacco instead of bubble gum, and it was a time before the superstars and the multi million-dollar contracts. It was a time when I played my heart out because I was just plain having fun and a time when I would have run head first over the creek bank in pursuit of a foul ball just to hear one of my teammates say, "Nice try."

If we'd kept batting averages, a record of errors and other stats, no one would have wanted me on their team. But we didn't, so seldom did anyone fail to pick me because I wasn't much of a glove man or had fewer RBI than someone else.

Consequently, I can remember with pleasure, and talk about my ball-playing days with a pride equal to that of the best-pitching, fastest-running and slickest-fielding Muddy Brancher of my day. And not only did we not keep stats, we seldom kept score, either. Scoring another run would simply mean we'd keep bats longer. Oh sure, someone would always attempt to keep track of who had how many runs, but it wasn't really official or anything.

"Is that 27 or 28?" someone would ask.

"No, Dummy, that's only 26," someone else would answer. "Remember, Jimmy made an out. They's two outs, you know."

"You're crazy! They's just one. That was last inning. Jimmy ain't batted this time, have you, Jimmy?"

"I don't remember," Jimmy would say.

He didn't remember because it didn't matter. You see, no one ever lost because no one ever won. When it came to baseball, I was a superstar and was just as great as I imagined myself to be.

• • •

One of the best all-around baseball players in our group was Eck Sparks. I was 12, he was 14 and I listened with envy as he told me how he had "made the baseball team" at Meade Memorial High School where he had just enrolled as a freshman.

It was in early September and one evening a group of us had played baseball until it had gotten so dark we could hardly see each other, let alone the ball. Sweaty and tired we had walked home amid the "catch ya later" and "see ya tomorrow" farewells, as one by one each player would come to his house.

The next morning, the first thing Mom said to me was, "Eck's dead."

To me that was impossible. Just yesterday we had played ball together. He was fine. He couldn't be dead.

But he was.

His appendix had ruptured during the night and he died before they could get him to the hospital.

Eck's death literally devastated me. I had seen lots of dead people: old people or not-so-old people who had been killed in the war or in the mines. But not someone just like me. I remember that they ran a school bus from Meade School so that Eck's fellow students could attend his funeral at the Thealka Free Will Baptist Church.

It was during that funeral service that I decided that Eck's fate would also be my own. I believed, without a shadow of a doubt, that when I became 14, I too would die of appendicitis.

I would lie awake listening to the night sounds and picture how it would be. How everybody would cry and say what a good boy I'd been. How all my friends would sit up with me and eat sandwiches from Mom's kitchen table. How Charley "Rat" Bailey would preach my funeral. How he would preach me right into Heaven.

I was so convinced of my impending death at age 14 that no future plans ever went beyond that time. As a matter of fact, about a week before I was to enter high school, I imagined myself with a case of appendicitis so real that Dad and Mom took me to the doctor. Dr. Hall mashed around on my stomach and I spent the night in the Paintsville Hospital. (The only time I was ever hospitalized until I was 55 years old and had a bout with high blood pressure.)

Anyway, the next morning a nurse came in and told me I could go home because blood tests had shown that I had absolutely nothing wrong with me.

I guess the fact that the people at the hospital couldn't find anything wrong with me sort of helped end my fear. The various activities of my freshman year at Meade completely drowned out my preoccupation with death, and quite suddenly, I turned 15.

• • •

As I've stated throughout this book, the folks who lived in Thealka in the 1940s were, by and large, good, hard-working, God-fearing people. Yet, I don't want to leave the impression that every last one of them was perfect. Be assured that, just like every other society anywhere, we had our warts.

For example, Trail Lee Wallace, whose wife had taken their children and moved to Michigan (I never knew why, because if someone was talking about it and I came into the room, they hushed), was nowhere near perfect. Trail was a tall, skinny, hard-working miner during the day, and was well-known for his drinking at night and on weekends. To be more exact, since drinking was frowned upon in the community, he was considered by everybody who knew him to be a drunk, a lush, a pure sot. Furthermore, it was Trail's whiskey drinking that nearly prompted a bunch of us boys (who, although we didn't know it at the time, were merely practicing the art of recycling almost 50 years before it became fashionable) to partake in the evils of drinking ourselves. Now don't misunderstand; it wasn't intentional on his part or anything. It just kind of happened.

You see, when he'd finish a bottle, he'd step out onto his back porch and fling it into the pile of old tin cans that had accumulated in the back lane behind his house. And, since raising our show fares was chiefly dependant upon our ability to gather pop bottles and pieces of scrap iron, many of us frequented Trail Lee's pile of tin cans on a regular basis.

One day when several of us were poking around looking for whatever might be turned into some quick cash, Paul VanHoose noticed that practically every whiskey bottle still intact had about half a swallow left in it and when he'd hold the bottle just right, it'd drain down and fill the corner with a little amber-colored triangle. Furthermore, practically every one of the bottles had been recorked before they'd been thrown away.

"I got a good idea," Paul said. "Let's get all those liquor bottles and take them to the clubhouse." (Our clubhouse was two or three pieces of old roofing tin that we'd nailed at an angle to the corner of our smokehouse and covered with a discarded linoleum rug.)

When somebody asked why, Paul said, "Just do it. I'll show you why."

We did, and what he showed us was that if we'd pour all the half-swallows of whiskey into just one bottle, before long we could have us a whole half-pint.

We put our plan into action and met every day after school to gather up the empties and drain their remains into our bottle. In order to measure our progress, we even put little pencil marks on the edge of the bright yellow label of the bottle we were attempting to fill, much like we'd have done to the door facing if we had been measuring our height.

We worked diligently, paying no attention to the various brands. Every drop we could find went into that one bottle, and after what seemed like forever, but was probably no more than two or three weeks, our bottle would hold no more.

We were one proud bunch as we passed it around and held it at arm's length for inspection.

"What now?" one of us asked.

"Now we drink it, silly," another answered.

"Not me," someone else protested. "This stuff's got every kind of whiskey in the world in it, even gin and vodkie. It'd kill every blessed one of us. I wouldn't drink it if someone held a gun on me."

"I know, let's sell it."

"We can't do that. They'd railroad us for boot-leggin'."

After much high-level discussion led to no agreeable solution, we decided to hide the bottle in a little nook beneath the smokehouse, think about it and meet later to decide its fate.

In the 1940s, though, Muddy Branch was one exciting place and, to say the least, our interests were varied. Before long, thoughts of the world's strangest half-pint of whiskey waned and were replaced by some other devious plan. As a matter of fact, I had personally forgotten about our stash until one day when I was looking for pop bottles in the pile of tin cans behind Trail Lee's house. It was then I noticed the empty whiskey bottle with the strange little pencil markings on its bright yellow label.

To this day I don't know if Trail Lee had been watching us and helped himself to our strange concoction when we weren't looking, or if he'd bought the bottle from one of my cohorts who'd decided to turn a slick profit with a one-way split.

Either way, it seems that one Mr. Trail Lee Wallace not only had the last laugh, but also enjoyed his liquor, right down to the last drop.

• • •

Ninety percent of our play time was spent outside. That's why in the summer of 1992, I made a special trip to my old stomping grounds in the head of Silk Stocking Row. The primary purpose of my visit was to see if our big sycamore tree was still standing in front of the old dairy barn after nearly 50 years.

It was.

It's funny, though, how time has a way of making things shrink. Not only have the houses in Society Row gotten smaller and closer together, but the size of everything else seems to have diminished, too. When I was five or six years old, three of us could hide behind that old sycamore and never be seen as we played hide-and-seek or kick-the-can. Now, I doubt that I alone could conceal myself behind it. The girth of one of either the tree or me surely must have changed.

That tree must be at least a hundred years old, and it certainly looked it. It appeared almost battle-scarred with its bark all dark and scaly. Its branches didn't seem as strong and healthy-looking, nor its leaves as plentiful as I remembered. To me this old tree was a giant umbrella and many's the time we continued playing under it during a summer rain with hardly a drop reaching us.

Of course, if the "old tater wagon" began to roll (that's how we referred to thunder), we'd either head for home or take cover in the old dairy barn a few yards away. The barn's not there now.

The kids in the neighborhood always referred to the big sycamore as "our tree" because it was beneath its branches we'd gather on those long, hot summer afternoons. The girls had lots of flat, grassless spots on which to draw their hopscotch lines. They'd hunt a flat rock to toss or use a perfectly round, milky-white piece of glass taken from those old Mason jar lids. (After I became an adult I became curious about that game. What the girls were tossing were called "pucks." We just called them little rocks and pieces of glass.)

There was also room in the cool shade of the grand tree for the boys to have a dandy diamond on which to play "burn out." Sometimes the games got in the way of each other, but if one of the girls had been hit with a line drive it wouldn't have been serious because we only played with old tennis balls and used an old mop handle or broomstick for a bat. We played burn out using baseball rules, except for two differences. One, you got only one swing at the ball. Whether you hit it or not, you ran for first base. The second difference was how you made an out: the opposing players could throw the ball at you. That included the catcher, who was usually the oldest player and hardest thrower on the other team. I never played the game unless I had a shirt on. I didn't want to risk catching an old tennis ball between my shoulder blades, especially if the ball had gotten wet.

One of our dads had tied a thick, sea grass rope to an overhanging branch of the big sycamore and made us a swing. It was a good one, too, and we enjoyed seeing how high we could make it go. Swinging on it was really quite a thrill, especially the descent, because if we really tried, we could make someone go ten or twelve feet high.

One day we made Libby Ann Green go that high and just as we shoved her, one of the biggest black snakes I had ever seen fell from the high branches above the swing and landed slap in her lap. As the swing reached its highest point, she bailed out. There was plenty of room for her to land, too, because those of us close enough to have seen what happened took off like scalded cats.

Anyway, Libby Ann hit the ground running and screaming like a Comanche. I don't know where she went, but the snake slithered for the culvert at the edge of the play area. It got away, despite the manly efforts of us brave boys, who chased and threw gravels at it, from a safe distance, of course. Had my brother Ernest been there, though, he'd have had it in his hip pocket in nothing flat. He was a really good snake catcher.

In 1992, however, as I looked through faded memories and through adult eyes, things were not the same, and I felt really strange as I stood beneath the aged branches of our tree. My head was full of fifty-year-old memories of young, happy faces; lazy, laughter-filled afternoons; and innocent children's games.

• • •

And speaking of trees as being a reminder that change comes all too rapidly, another occurred when Wilma and I lazed away the Sunday afternoon on our back deck a couple of Septembers ago. It was an absolutely perfect day and we couldn't help but notice that there was something a bit different in the way the breezes played the two wind chimes hanging just out of arm's length in one of the three pine trees that Todd and I had planted more than 20 years earlier.

We'd carried the three puny-looking sprigs with their hairlike roots all the way from Louisville, where they had been put into individual plastic bags and placed on banquet tables at the Galt House.

We were there because Todd, then a fifth grader, had won a state conservation poster contest. No doubt inspired by messages he'd heard from environmentalists that weekend, he insisted we set the plants out as soon as we got home. With a long screwdriver I poked three small holes in the earth not 20 feet from our back door and stuck the plants into them. Not believing for a second that the scrawny twigs would survive in the rocky soil, yet feeling compelled to say something over such a major event as a father and his son planting a tree, I said, "By the time you're a grown man, these will be tall trees."

Am I a prophet or what? As he matured, so did they. Now, much too close to the house, they stand a good 40 feet high and, other than reminding us that time passes way too quickly, serve no other purpose than to hold the wind chimes that now scattered ceaseless, yet untied, musical notes above our heads all afternoon.

Actually, the breeze that day was different more for what it meant than for what it was. While it was comfortable, even refreshing, in its coolness, Wilma and I both knew it meant that in a few weeks the surrounding forests would deem it necessary to change their wardrobe from faded greens to yellow and orange hues, then settle for a few days upon the drab monochromatic brown before shedding their clothes altogether.

A fragile hummingbird visited briefly and pulled nectar from the yellow center of the single begonia that sat atop the deck rail not six feet away from where we sat thumbing through the Sunday paper. Even it could not have failed to sense that the genteelness of the afternoon was a mere harbinger of sister breezes to follow in less than a month as our friends from Canada sent their cold air masses this way.

I suppose of the four seasons, Wilma and I both like autumn best. I kid her that she's fond of it simply because that's when she got me. She insists that she still loves fall in spite of that.

All joking aside (at least I hope she was joking), there was indeed something in the air that day that silently screamed change. And of course, that's all fitting and proper, too, for what else on earth is any more certain than that nothing stays the same.

· · ·

Libby Ann and Joe were the same age and pretty much the same size. As six-year-olds they played together a good deal and fought constantly.

Libby Ann had blond, curly hair and was tomboyish. When she and Joe fought, it was on equal terms and seldom was either victorious.

Anyway, one day Dad had decided he'd "had enough squabbling," and told them both they just had to get along better or he would fix them good.

Neither knew what the "fix-them-good" part of his threat meant and in a day or two, they got into it again; a real hair-

Libby Ann Green and Joe. They fought on equal terms.

pulling, clawing, rolling-around-in-the-dirt kind of "squabble," so Dad pulled them apart, took one by each hand and led them over to the edge of the porch. He sat down and put Libby Ann on one side of him and Joe on the other.

"Now I told you about that fighting," he said. "I want you to kiss and make up."

They both started to jump up and run but he held them firmly and told them that he wasn't kidding.

He made Joe kiss Libby Ann on the cheek and finally coaxed her to kiss him back.

They continued playing together, but they never fought again...while Dad was around.

But they did share a frightening experience along about that time when they got run over by one of Sonny Stafford's young colts which, along with four or five full-grown horses, was being chased up the back lane by a bunch of boys. As the small herd, in full gallop, rounded the corner of Claude VanHoose's backyard fence, Libby Ann and Joe, who were not even aware that the horses were around until the very last second, were too slow in removing themselves from their path and were sent sprawling into a big mud hole.

Fortunately, things looked a lot worse than they were and after the dirt and grime and a trickle or two of blood were washed away, it appeared that neither of them had been stepped on. Neither was really hurt, except for a few bruises that vanished as cool autumn days turned into winter and drove us all indoors.

Chapter VII
Moving Up

As was usually the case with whatever new thing that came along, the Packs were among the last families in Society Row to get a telephone. I'm not sure whether Dad just simply didn't see a need to have one or whether he felt paying a telephone bill every month was just an expense we couldn't afford.

But when phones moved into Society Row, several of our neighbors went on line, so to speak. At first, there was probably one phone for every four or five houses, and it was not uncommon to see people standing around on a neighbor's porch waiting their turn to use the phone. I've no idea who it was they were calling.

Then, we finally got one and for quite a while it was a real novelty. And never let it be said that coal-camp kids didn't know what to do with a novelty.

Sometimes when a bunch of us would get together, I'd disguise my voice and call down to the commissary and ask if they had Prince Albert in a can. If the person on the other end answered in the affirmative, I'd say, "Well, let him out. He'll smother." Or, I'd call someone I didn't know and ask if their refrigerator was running. If they said "yes", I'd say, "Well, you better run and catch it."

Boy, was that funny, or what?

However, when I was caught participating in such shenanigans, Dad had a tendency to become more than a little upset.

"I'm gonna have that thing taken out if you boys don't stop aggravating people," he'd say.

But, being an obvious slow learner, I didn't stop. Consequently, I'm afraid that the way Dad reached out and touched me was not exactly what Ma Bell had in mind.

There had been a time when, if a person had to make a phone call, he would go to the Northeast Coal Company store. Of course, those kinds of calls were usually emergencies, like calling a taxi for a ride to town, or calling the doctor when someone got really sick.

However, even when everyone who wanted a phone had one, it still proved a little difficult to make a call sometimes. You see, the party-line system was in effect, with perhaps a half-dozen homes sharing the same line. Of course, if you had an emergency, all you had to do was interrupt the conversation and ask for the line. You'd better believe, though, that the party you infringed upon would be listening, and your emergency better have been genuine. Otherwise, never again would they get off so that you could get on.

Anybody on your line could listen in any time they wanted to because when someone called somebody, the phone rang in the other homes, too. Everyone knew who was getting a call because the phones rang in code. Our ring was two longs and two shorts. Someone else had two shorts and a long. Three shorts; one long, one short; one long; four shorts, and so on.

I often heard complaints about nosy neighbors sharing the lines, but we were fortunate enough not to be bothered with extra listeners unless the call came late at night or really early in the morning. People felt that these calls were very serious and they kindled more interest on down the line.

You finished this type of call something like this: "Okay, Bob. Thanks a lot. 'Bye."

Click...click...click, click, click, Hmmmmmmmmmmmmm.

Sometimes I miss those old phones. They weren't dial or push-button; you just picked up the receiver and waited for the operator to say, "Number, please?"

Phone numbers then weren't hard to remember like they are now. We had none of these area codes, and stuff like that. For example, our number was 27-W. Someone else on our party line was 27-J; someone else, 27-R. When the operator asked for it, you'd just say it and she'd just ring it.

More than once I gave the operator the number I wished to call and she said, "They're not home. They've gone to church." On other occasions, while she was ringing the number, she asked how my mother was.

Local operators then were local operators.

• • •

One invention that was not new was radio. I'm sure my family owned a radio long before I was born. I'm equally sure that not another member of the family enjoyed that radio as much as I did.

Radio listening then was primarily a nocturnal activity because the moms and dads spent their daytimes working, and the kids were always, except in the dead of winter, playing outdoors.

My imagination painted bright pictures of those far-away places with the strange sounding names as I spent night after night with folks like Edgar Bergen, Charlie McCarthy and Mortimer Snerd, who had become very good friends of mine.

It was from radio, too, that I learned to love a mystery. I tagged along with Jack, Doc and Reggie as they solved crime after crime. I also shared many adventures with Jack Armstrong, all-American boy.

I'd find Jack at WBBM in Chicago, which most of the time had a good clear signal. He was this high school kid who looked a whole lot like me. (That's another thing that radio had over television. The actors looked just like whomever you imagined).

Anyway, Jack Armstrong would get into all kinds of scrapes with everyone from schoolyard bullies to German spies (remember, there was a war going on) and he always came out on top. When the show would come on, a squad of cheerleaders would be chanting Jack's school song. I can still remember how it went: "Wave the flag for Hudson High, show them how we stand. Something ... something ... something ... something ... known across the land."

Well, I almost remembered it.

One reason for Jack Armstrong's success, of course, was his secret whistle code. Only his closest pals, like Joe and me, knew that one short whistle meant we needed to pay attention, and two short whistles meant we'd better be very careful. What we dreaded hearing, though, but did with every episode, was one long and two short whistles. That meant our hero was in dire straits.

I guess you might say that this show was sort of a soap opera for kids. Only the sponsor wasn't selling soap, it was selling Wheaties. Which, quite naturally, was only fitting since Wheaties is the breakfast of champions and Jack Armstrong was certainly that. Ironically, I can't ever remember eating Wheaties when I was growing up. Corn flakes and puffed wheat, yes. Wheaties, no.

I was also a regular listener of "Beulah" and waited in anticipation as her boyfriend would come to call and tap out "shave and a haircut, two bits" on her door, followed by a deep voice saying, "It's Bill, baby, your great big bundle of love." As the live radio audience broke into uncontrolled laughter, so would

I. For the longest time, I didn't realize that Beulah was a black lady. Although black families lived in other coal camps throughout Eastern Kentucky, there were none in Thealka and the first black person I ever saw was when I was about eight years old and a black preacher came one summer to the Thealka Free Will Baptist Church to hold a revival.

I was listening to the radio as boxing champion Joe Louis fought and defeated Jersey Joe Walcott in a far-off place called Madison Square Garden, and I sat right there in the White House with President Roosevelt as he chatted before his fire. I didn't really understand all he said, but I do remember wondering who'd chopped his wood, toted in his coal and built his fire for him.

I still remember the voice of Randy Blake at WJJD, also in Chicago, as he played records like Tex Ritter's "Jack-O-Diamonds" on the "Suppertime Frolic," and thanks to long-ago radio, little jingles like "Halo, everybody, Halo," still pop into my head from time to time whenever I wash my hair.

When TV came along, as marvelous as it was, it kind of spoiled some of those images that were slowly burned into my mind as I sat staring at the soft yellow light behind the radio dial and listening to "Our Miss Brooks" and "Amos and Andy" (I did know that Amos and Andy were black, but it was years before I discovered the actors portraying them weren't). Eve Arden didn't look much like the Miss Brooks in my mind, nor did Amos and the Kingfish look like my Amos and my Kingfish. I liked mine better in all three cases.

Some of my early radio memories took on a somber tone, too, because during World War II, the late-afternoon editions of Gabriel Heatter and the news always brought a hush around the house. This was important stuff because Ulysses and Hubert were in the war. They were both in the Navy and Mom and

Hubert, Mom, and me a few days after Hubert came home from the Navy.

Dad knew the names of the ships they were on. I can remember Dad, still wearing his dirty bank clothes, sitting motionless in front of the fire with his head in his hands for the full 15-minute broadcast which always included the names of American ships sunk by the Japanese.

Fortunately, they never heard the names for which they listened, because both Ulysses and Hubert got home okay.

It seems that the older I get, the more faded those radio signals become. But, one reason that my memories as the son of a coal miner are happy ones was because the sound of radio, fueled by an overactive imagination, carried me each night beyond the world of reality to a magical land filled with music, laughter and adventure.

• • •

Just as with the telephone, Dad was also slow in getting us a television. But when he did, it was a 17-inch Crosley, black and white, of course.

Back then, when one bought a TV, one also bought an antenna and hundreds of feet of wire. The wire was a double strand of thin copper separated every six inches or so with a clear plastic piece about an inch long and about as round as a pencil. Somebody told us once that the sound came through one wire and the picture through the other. We had no reason to doubt them because sometimes we'd have a picture with no sound and other times we'd have sound with no picture. The wire came in rolls about three feet in diameter and was very, very heavy.

The antenna was not of the roof-top variety, either, like I had seen in a Norman Rockwell painting on the front of a *Saturday Evening Post*; that would have been a snap. Ours was very bulky, unfolded to be six or seven feet long, and had to be mounted on a metal pipe about eight feet long, then placed in the top of a tall tree. Of course, the tree had to be on top of the highest hill nearest our house. We pointed the antenna as close as possible toward Huntington, West Virginia, because WSAZ was the only station we could pick up.

So, when we got our set, Dad and I, with Joe tagging along, spent the better part of the day lugging the wire and antenna to the very top of the hill in front of our house. Risking nosebleed, and after dozens of complicated verbal instructions from the ground, I mounted the antenna to the top of a tall hickory, or at least that's what Dad said it was. Then we chopped through the brambles, bushes and briars to clear a path between trees on which we mounted the brackets and hung the wire.

A couple of hours later, when we finally reached the house and got everything hooked up, we held our collective breaths as we turned it on and switched to channel three. After several seconds of warming up, our living room was filled with a soft-blue glow. By now, two or three of the neighbors had gathered to see what kind of picture we had. As it came into focus, someone commented, "Clear as a glass jug." We were in business.

Everything would go along pretty well until there was a rain or snow or wind. Then, right smack in the middle of "Mr. Peepers" or "Death Valley Days," we'd suddenly find ourselves staring at a snow-filled screen.

Usually the problem was nothing more than a piece of brush that had fallen on the line and was simple to remedy; however, more often than not, the brush had fallen much closer to the antenna than the house. Also, more often than not, it fell upon me to "run the line," because Dad would say, "You do it, Clyde. You're on your first set of legs."

Chapter VIII
Coal-Camp Cuisine

I feel fortunate, maybe even blessed, that I've never been addicted to cigarettes or alcohol and I've never smoked dope. Nevertheless, I can attest to the pain and confusion of suddenly stopping the consumption of something upon which my body had become dependent. I guess this particular affliction could be common among coal-camp kids, but when I went off to college, my body was shocked into withdrawal when I suddenly stopped eating bologna.

You see, when I was growing up, we probably ate more bologna than anything else, next to soup beans, of course. We ate bologna with eggs and gravy for breakfast, and we ate bologna sandwiches or bologna with crackers all during the day. Of course, the primary reason (besides it being just plain good) was that it was so inexpensive. Gene Miller, who ran the company store, would cut a hunk that would weigh half a pound from a big roll for 35 or 40 cents.

Regardless of what the cute little boy with the fishing pole used to say on the TV commercial, our bologna did not have a first name. However, it did have a nickname or two. Just as those good ole soup beans were called "miners' strawberries," we called bologna "miner's steak."

"What kinda sandwich ya eatin'?"

"Steak."

"Miner's steak?"

"Yep."

Sometimes folks would call it "dear meat," as in "dear ole bologna," or even "dog meat." I don't even want to try to guess why. But regardless of what you called it, a big bologna sandwich with mustard, tomato, and a slice of onion, washed down with a cold bottle of pop or a glass of strawberry Kool-Aid, was the menu for lunch most days. On those rare occasions when we were out of bologna, we'd settle for a mustard or mayonnaise sandwich. We also ate of lot of jelly sandwiches. Sometimes, we'd just spread catsup between two slices of bread and eat that. As the beer commercial says, "It just doesn't get any better than this."

Speaking of commercials, a favorite memory of my early days at the H. S. Howes Community School concerns an advertisement for a soft drink. I'm not talking radio, and certainly not TV, for at that time I'd never even seen one of those. I'm talking skywriting.

The familiar drone of the plane was unmistakable and whenever an alert spotter on the way to the bathroom would notice the airplane, he'd forget he had to go, if indeed he really did, and run and tell Mr. Chandler. Probably thinking we could all stand a diversion, Mr. Chandler would ring the bell and the entire student body, all eight grades, would be dismissed to the paper-filled school yard to gaze heavenward . We'd watch the tiny speck of a biplane spell out, in towering smoke letters, P...E...P...S...I, and we'd stand for 30 or 40 minutes and watch until the smoke dissipated into shapeless white puffs, or until our necks would get cricks in them, whichever came first.

Anyway, the sad thing about my suffering all these withdrawal pains and stuff the first few weeks that I was away from home, was that I had no idea what was the matter with me. At first I thought it was homesickness. I'd heard all sorts of stories about how awful that was, but when I started waking up in a cold sweat after dreaming I was reaching for a big bologna sandwich that would suddenly disappear, I put two and two together and figured out what was wrong.

• • •

In the summertime, thanks to a lot of hard work on Dad's part, we ate a lot of fresh corn on the cob. We called them "roshineers" and I'll admit I was sort of surprised when I learned that *roshineers* wasn't even a word.

I was sitting in a health class in the old Weaver Building on the campus of Eastern Kentucky State College in the fall of 1957 and the class was discussing the basic food groups. When corn was mentioned, I casually mentioned that I loved roshineers. I might just as well have been speaking in a foreign tongue, because everybody just kind of stared at me like they had no earthly idea of what I'd just said. I tried to explain, "You know, roshineers. Corn. Corn on the cob."

Our teacher (we called her "old Lady Hood" because Hood was her last name) told me I meant "roasting ears."

"No, you don't roast them, you boil them in water," I explained further.

Everybody laughed, except me. Personally, I felt sort of sorry for those kids from Louisville and southern Indiana and places like that who didn't know what a roshineer was.

Anyway, I thought I liked roshineers about as much as anybody could, until I married Wilma Jean. I've never seen a woman love roshineers like she does. I wouldn't be surprised if she fixed roshineers for breakfast some morning. Naw, that wouldn't work.

I think that now I'm retired from the classroom, I'll buy me a good team of mules and two or three acres of river bottom somewhere and raise Wilma tons of roshineers.

Of course, if some city slicker should drop by for supper (or should I raise my pinky finger and say *dinnah?*), I'll see if I can't rustle up a "roasting ear" for them. But between you and me and the gate post, roshineers are a lot better.

• • •

As an adult, I've never canned, or as my mom used to say, "put up food." But my mother did and so did practically every other woman who lived in Muddy Branch in the 1940s.

Even though the kitchen was usually a place for little boys to eat their meals, do their homework, or simply pass through on the way out the back door, canning was a family affair at our house, and I'd no doubt be wealthy today if I had a dime for every big-mouthed Mason jar I've washed.

Joe and I were too young to be much help otherwise, but it usually fell upon us to help Mom wash those tons of jars that had been accumulating in the corner of the smoke house for the past year, and I'll never forget how much trouble we'd have getting those rust rings from the grooves in the neck of those things. No matter how much we'd scrub and scald, if Mom would see one speck of brown, and she was a thorough in-spector, back into the soak tub it'd go, and we'd have to do it all over again. At least once in every wash session, one of us would say, "We eat what we can and what we can't eat we can," and the other one would giggle. Then Mom would tell us to stop playing and get to work.

Anyway, no matter how hard or how long we'd wash, it seemed as if that pile of dirty jars would never get any smaller because when Dad raised a garden, Dad raised a garden. He'd work until dark nearly every day after he'd get home from the mines, and by canning time he'd have enough vegetables to feed half the neighborhood, which is exactly what he'd do.

I guess I was too young, but as I'd help him carry bucket after bucket of tomatoes, corn, cucumbers, green beans and cabbage heads to give to the older neighbors, or those who had large families, I had difficulty understanding his Christian benevolence. However, when I'd face those dirty jars, I'd wish he'd have given more of it away than he had.

• • •

Another food staple at our house when I was growing up was eggs. I'll bet I ate at least one a day for the first 12 or 15 years of my life. Regardless of what else Mom fixed for breakfast, she nearly always fixed an egg to go with it. She'd boil them, scramble them, or fry them, leaving them a bit runny. On Sundays sometimes she'd devil them.

Not even on a double-dog dare have I ever eaten one raw. I'm glad, too, because I read in the paper once that the Center for Science in the Public Interest was suggesting that egg cartons should carry labels warning consumers that eating raw eggs—even in cookie or cake dough—can poison you.

I suppose I, and probably everybody else reared in like manner who might have licked the bowl wherein Mom had just mixed cake batter or eaten eggs that were a little runny, should consider ourselves lucky.

Since breakfast continues to be my favorite meal, though, I guess I'll just have to remember to say, "scramble 'em."

• • •

Since Dad always kept a good milk cow, we always had an ample supply of buttermilk. As a matter of fact, for a while we even sold milk and butter and buttermilk to some of the neighbors. Of course, when our cow was dry, we'd have to buy our dairy products from someone else in the community or, of course, from the company store.

I never knew anybody, young or old, who didn't like buttermilk, and many lunches or late-night snacks consisted of a big bowl of leftover cornbread covered with cold buttermilk. And for supper, you just couldn't beat a bowl of soup beans, a hunk of cornbread, a slice of onion and buttermilk.

Not anymore, though, and it's really too bad that today's kids don't seem to like buttermilk. They even snub their noses at the mere suggestion of it. In their defense, however, that could be because what's sold in the stores today is nothing more than a cheap imitation of the real thing.

We see advertisements on TV and in the newspapers all the time for canned buttermilk biscuits, buttermilk pancakes that come in a box and even buttermilk dressing to pour over salads. But there's not a coal-camp kid alive who doesn't know that real buttermilk doesn't come in a waxed-paper carton or a plastic jug. We know that real buttermilk comes from a churn that Mom used to sit next to the warm fireplace to clabber before she'd insert the wooden dasher and churn the butter to the top.

Maybe I'm getting old, but I can't help but associate drinking buttermilk with more peaceful, happier times when people had a certain unspoken respect, not only for each other, but for buttermilk, too. For example, Hoagy Carmichael wrote a hit song called "Old Buttermilk Sky," and Dale Evans even named her horse Buttermilk. Now what could be a better tribute than that?

Therefore, since I can't keep from associating buttermilk with a more easy-going, laid-back society, I wonder if the many problems we have now resulting from the pressures of our day-to-day lives wouldn't seem much less important if we'd all sit down and discuss them over a glass of buttermilk.

• • •

If you can believe what you read in the papers, not only is everything we eat not good for us, but dining itself has become very dull, even boring, because we're eating the same things all the time.

According to yet another governmental study—or at least the U.N. Food and Agriculture Organization sounds to me like it'd be something governmental—there are more than 50,000 species of edible plants, and we humans eat only about 300 of them. Furthermore, we only eat eight animal species and five species of birds.

While all this may be true, it's still hard for me to get excited about governmental studies. I remember when one of those scared everybody half to death about sugar. Remember when we were told that we ought to eat artificial sweeteners? You know, the "sweeteners" that were so bitter they'd turn your mouth inside out? Then, remember the governmental study that said that artificial sweeteners weren't good for you?

And remember when the study came out that said butter and eggs would kill you? And biscuits and gravy? And pork chops? And red meat? (Is bologna a red meat?) Remember when a study suggested that we all become vegetarians, then one followed shortly suggesting that since farmers were using poisonous chemicals to grow bigger and juicier fruits and vegetables, we'd better not eat so many fruits and vegetables?

Anyway, take it for what it's worth, this new study apparently not only warns us about boredom, but also about running out of stuff. It does offer some alternatives to pizza, spam and leg of lamb. The report says that there are hundreds of things left to eat that not only taste good, but are also good for us: things like oca, arrachacha, ollucha and carambola. Since I have no earthly notion as to what any of this stuff is, I can't personally recommend them.

It's not surprising to me, or anyone else who was reared in an Eastern Kentucky coal camp like Muddy Branch, but there are a couple of things that are indeed recognizable among all these recommendations: beans.

One is called the marama bean, which is supposed to have more protein than peanut butter and twice the oil of soybeans. The other is the adzuki bean. Apparently, the Japanese eat a lot of adzuki beans, and also use them in making pastries. Not only that, but they also use them to make a soft drink.

Again, since I've never tried them, I'd better not comment, except to say that I'd bet a nickel against the hole in a doughnut that neither of them would come close to being as good as the pinto and navy beans we enjoyed as kids, and still do, for that matter. (Soft drinks? Wonder what a bottle of soup bean pop would taste like? Wonder what it'd do for you? Would it make you belch, or...what?)

I'm sure that since they've spent so much of our money making these studies, they're sure to spend some more researching how best to package, present and sell all this to the public. So, while they're figuring it all out, I guess I'll just try to force myself to eat a few more boring meals of fried potatoes with a boring slab of cornbread and a slice of boring onion.

• • •

And while we're discussing coal-camp diet, let's not leave out potatoes.

Mostly we ate them fried. We called them "fried taters." On Sundays when Mom would fix fried chicken, she'd mash the potatoes. If she had a lot left over for supper, she'd shape them into cakes.

When I was really small we lived up Jim Dale Hollow and the house we lived in had a fireplace. Sometimes when we were sitting around at night listening to the "Suppertime Frolic" on WJJD, and were in an extremely festive mood, we'd bake them by burying them in the ashes under the grate. Most of the time, by the time we got off all the ash and stuff, there wasn't a whole lot of potato left.

The first potato chip I ever ate was homemade. I probably wasn't much older than seven or eight, but I remember my sister Mary Jean, my future sister-in-law Georgene and some more girls in Society Row all got together one night and sliced about a peck real thin, put them in a big black skillet, and deep-fried them in hog lard. Apparently, cholesterol hadn't been invented yet.

I don't remember whether I liked them or not, but since I've always had a tendency to enjoy anything edible, I probably did.

I can recall one occasion, however, when I didn't much enjoy potatoes.

Dad probably raised more potatoes in his garden than anything else. Once when he was digging them, Joe and I had the job of picking them up and putting them into bushel baskets. Joe was in front of me in the row below me, maybe about eight or ten feet away and when he wasn't looking, I sort of *gently* tossed a *tiny* potato in his direction and hit him in the back of the head.

He yelled like I had shot him and fired a *really big* one at me, hitting me in the back, since I'd seen it coming and had tried to duck. I wasn't wearing a shirt and it really stung. But being the good sport I was, and since I did start it, I let it go and went back to picking up potatoes. I'd no more started when WHAM, an even bigger one caught me right above my left ear. I'd just been kidding around, but Joe was really mad. He started throwing at me with a vengeance, and potatoes were flying past my head like a swarm of yellow jackets.

Fortunately, Dad was close by and intervened before Joe caused any permanent damage to his big brother.

Joe was slow to forget and another time when we'd been into it over something, he threw a hatchet at me as I stepped out of the kitchen door, a good two hours after the squabble was over. Fortunately, his aim with a hatchet was not as good as his aim with a potato. It didn't come close, but if it had found its mark, it probably would have killed me.

• • •

There was one instance, though, when, quite by accident, I became a genuine hero to Joe.

Bud Walters, who was just a little younger than me but a lot older than Joe, was known to enjoy a good fight and had every other kid his age and younger a little scared of him. Even I was in that number, sort of.

Every time Joe went out to play alone, Bud would whip him and he'd come home crying. On one such occasion, Mom jumped my case for not defending my "precious little brother," and came down so hard on me that I felt as if I had beaten him up instead of Bud. Anyway, I made up my mind that I'd catch Bud when he wasn't in a fighting mood and try to talk him into

Me and Joe. Don't know who owned the cow.

not beating up my little brother anymore.

An hour or two later, I saw Bud down in the creek near the culvert that ran under our play area beneath the big sycamore poking around, probably for a crawdad or waterdog, and I casually walked up to him and said, "Son, you'd better leave Joe alone."

I didn't mean to say that, and I sure didn't mean for it to come out as a challenge. But it did, and without a second's hesitation, he accepted it. He came at me like he was going to put me in a headlock or something and as I turned to get out of his way, I tripped over a big root that was growing on top of the ground and fell backward. As I did, I grabbed at him and, somehow, he fell, too, right on his face. The impact flattened his nose, and blood gushed everywhere. It was in his eyes, his mouth, even his hair. I thought I'd killed him and apparently, he did, too. We both ran home and I told Mom that I'd bloodied Bud's nose and I thought he was probably going to die. She said she'd go down and check on him (he only lived four houses below us) and when she got back she said Bud's mom said that he was okay, that his nose bled all the time and not to worry about it.

But for two or three days, I was Joe's big hero and Bud Walters never bothered him again.

• • •

I was probably no more than eight or ten years old when I heard ole Gene Autry in one of his movies singing about you getting a line and me getting a pole all going fishing in the crawdad hole. I guess I remembered it all these years because I could identify with it. Crawdads were as much a part of life back then as were mustard sandwiches, kick-the-can and going barefoot in the summertime.

You see, crawdad tails were considered excellent bait to use when fishing for sundads in the Number One Pond.

And that was fortunate.

What made it so fortunate was that crawdads were easy to catch and it was nearly as much fun catching them as it was catching the sundads. Besides, digging fishworms was too much like work, especially when they were so hard to find in those hot, dry, dog-day summers of the 1940s. But the little creek (as far as I knew, it didn't have a name but ran into Boyd Branch just below Vencil Nelson's house) that ran behind the houses in Society Row was flat full of crawdads.

Two or three of us boys (most of the girls who lived in Society Row were too scared to touch them) could catch a dozen or so in no time—provided, of course, that we didn't get distracted by a good-size waterdog or a big chub minnow.

I can't imagine how I'd have reacted had I known that some people down in southern Louisiana and Texas actually had crawdad farms and raised them to sell to fancy restaurants; that people who called themselves connoisseurs would suck tiny bits of meat from the crawdad's claws and orange stuff they called "butter" from the crawdad's head. Yuk!

As an adult, I've eaten all kinds of seafood and, on a double-dog dare, even ate raw oysters once. I don't think I'll ever be persuaded to eat a crawdad, though.

• • •

When I left home and went to college, good eating places were a rarity and when I didn't eat in the cafeteria, I always made it a point to look for restaurants that featured signs in the window that read "Home Cooking," striving (in vain) to find someone, somewhere, who knew exactly how Mom fried her chicken. Today's generation of kids snub their nose at what today's moms fixes (when she fixes) and complains because hers isn't as good as the Colonel's.

I'll have to admit, though, that one thing all the different eateries of today provide that Mom didn't is variety. For example, I love pizza, but I was in college before I tasted it for the first time. My roommate kept talking about it and finally brought some to the dorm. As he served it up, he told me it was one of those foods that nobody liked at first and that you had to acquire a taste for. He was wrong.

I am, however, trying to acquire a taste for some of the Mexican food that is becoming so popular. Some of it is as difficult for me to digest as it is to pronounce. When I was growing up, I ate plenty of day-old beans, but we never, ever refried them.

• • •

And finally, how could I not mention how much we loved walnuts?

An ancient black walnut tree stood on the bank near the drawbars that led to the Slaughter Pen Hollow pasture. In the fall, when the tree had dropped its early-falling leaves and stood naked in its deeply furrowed, diamond patterned, dark brown bark with its heavily-laden limbs dropping fruit onto the little dirt road beneath it, I'd join a group of neighborhood kids in collecting, hulling, and cracking them.

The best tree climber in the bunch would usually ascend to the upper branches and shake the smaller limbs. The nuts we couldn't shake off, we'd knock off. We knew it would be useless to throw rocks, so we'd gather up heavy pieces of old lumber, climb the bank, and fling them into the tree. Sometimes nothing fell to the ground except the board we'd flung. On occasion, though, our efforts would bring forth a dozen or so of the green, tennis-ball-size nuts.

In short order, many of the young entrepreneurs who had less than half an hour before figured out a way to earn at least a month's worth of show fare from selling their share of the bountiful harvest, would lose interest in the project and wander off to some other distraction. I'd end up with half a bushel, or so, that I'd take home to dry out on top of the little lean-to shed attached to the smoke house.

After a few frosts had visited the camp, the hulls would turn black. I'd peel them, then put the nuts out to dry again. Hulling was one of those jobs that had to be done manually, so usually my hands remained stained a dark brown for weeks.

When I had absolutely nothing else to do, I'd gather the nuts which, after having been stripped of their hulls had diminished to the size of golf balls, would barely fill up more than a quarter of the bushel basket. There was a big flat rock near the edge of our back yard and, with the help of Dad's claw hammer, I'd settle there for an hour or so and crack the walnuts. This was the most difficult part of the operation because the nut was so hard that if I didn't hit it just right, it'd squib away. Plus, because I had to hold it so tightly to keep it from squibbing, sometimes little fingers would get in the way.

Anyway, after that, the most tedious part of the operation was at hand. I'd take a hair pin and pick out the kernels so Mary Jean could stir them into chocolate fudge. That's when all the time and effort involved in walnut harvesting really paid off.

CHAPTER IX

An Interesting Cast

My memories of growing up are filled with an interesting cast of characters: people who, although I didn't know it at the time, made my life truly interesting and well worth remembering nearly 60 years later.

Archie VanHoose was one such individual. Even though he was an adult, I called him Archie. I wouldn't have thought of calling him Mr. VanHoose because, even though he had five kids of his own, he was the type of fellow who was never too busy to spend some time with members of the younger generation. I guess I sort of considered him one of us.

Archie wore a permanent grin and was a well-known fox hunter. I really enjoyed sitting around on his back porch listening to him talk about Old Lead, his favorite hound, or about the time he took a willow switch and drove a swarm of bees from Louisa to Paintsville (a good 30 miles as the crow flies), losing only four bees along the way.

"I wouldn't have lost them," he'd say, "if it hadn't come a hail storm."

Although I'd never been fox hunting, when ole Arch would talk about it, I could almost believe that I was back in the woods at two in the morning, listening to those dogs myself. I'd get chills all over when he'd blow his cow horn or talk about how Old Lead would call on track or how Belle was always first to trail. I wasn't quite sure what he meant by all that, but I let on like I did.

One time I asked him how, since he had three or four dogs and since he always went hunting with three or four other men who also had three or four dogs, he could tell which dog was which by just listening.

"Son," he said, "if a man had ten kids, he'd still know which one was hollerin'. No hound sings as sweet as Old Lead."

Made sense to me. So did the part he told us about how a good dog could always recognize its master's call when the dog's owner would blow his horn.

"Someone else could blow all night," he'd say, "and my dogs wouldn't pay a bit of attention. As soon as I blow 'er, though, here they come."

Apparently, he didn't blow his horn every time he hunted because he often complained how one of his hounds had gotten lost over on Teays Branch or somewhere.

I guess Eastern Kentucky fox hunters don't really hunt foxes. Mostly what they do, as far as I can tell, is build a big fire back in the woods, drink black coffee, and listen to their dogs run.

Now, I don't remember exactly who was with me on one particular day, but it could have been Joe or Archie's boy Henry Cecil or Keith Lyons or Jimmy Spencer or Tucker Daniel or any combination of same, or even *all* of same. Anyway, I do remember that it was a hot day and we were kind of laid back in the shade on Archie's back porch listening to him, when someone said, "Boy, it's a hot 'un, ain't it?"

That's all the cue Archie needed and he said, "I'll tell ya, boys, I want to cry every time we have a day like this. It reminds me of Old Beck."

"Who's Old Beck?" asked an unsuspecting straightman.

"Why, Old Beck was the best mule I ever had, and I lost her on a day just like this, years ago."

"What do you mean, you lost her? Did she run off or something?"

"She died, son. She died."

"She died?"

"She died."

"How come?"

"Well, I was way back in the head of Well Hollow, way back on the side of the hill above Willie Arms' house, and I had Old Beck plowing my popcorn patch."

We could tell something was coming because when he had a good one, even though his expression would never change, his eyes would seem to sparkle.

"Well," he went on, "it was probably just a little hotter than it is now—must have been 110 in the shade—because all at once that popcorn started popping and Old Beck looked up, thought it was snowing, and laid right down in the middle of that popcorn patch...and froze to death. It was the most pitiful sight I'd ever seen in my life."

• • •

Archie was not only an entertaining talker and an avid fox hunter, but he was also the neighborhood beekeeper.

His backyard was well landscaped with flowering bushes and always buzzing with four or five bee gums. When word got around that he was getting ready to rob one of them, it usually attracted a crowd of curious on-lookers, mostly barefoot and shirtless little boys.

I always thought Archie to be extremely brave for when he'd harvest the honey, although he always wore a hood made of what looked like screen wire, he never wore gloves.

Once he talked me into smoking his bees while he lifted the top off the gum. He gave me this bellows-like thing filled with burning rags and showed me how to pump it so the smoke would come out good. He said they wouldn't sting me if I made plenty of smoke and didn't seem afraid.

Archie VanHoose and his wife, Jessie. All the kids in the neighborhood, especially the boys, really enjoyed Archie's tall tales.

I let him down on the latter, but I must have been a pretty good bee smoker because I didn't get stung. Many of my bare-backed buddies did, though. While I was laying the smoke to the bees, I could hear a yelp now and then from some of those standing at a "safe distance."

I remember that after we got through, Archie raked off a 10-pound lard bucket full of fresh honey for me to take home.

• • •

I didn't have to look too far to meet some very unforgettable characters. Like my little brother, for instance, as illustrated in the story of the time he tried to kill me with a hatchet, and again when he nearly caused Dad to kill me.

As is typical of dads, even today, it was not uncommon for a miner to spend his Saturdays doing odd jobs around the house, like replacing a broken window, repairing a torn screen door or painting the front porch swing.

On this particular day Dad decided to repair a leak in the

middle of the kitchen that had been pestering Mom. Because the lowest part of the roof was a good 10 or 12 feet high and was very steep, Dad wouldn't let Joe and me on top of the house. But, we helped him by handing up the bucket of tar, his little box of roofing nails and his hammer.

As he settled into the chore of locating the hole, Joe and I made ourselves comfortable beneath the weeping willow in the corner of the yard where we could watch and be handy if Dad needed anything. After a few minutes, though, Joe, as was his nature, got bored with it all and wandered off.

After about half an hour, Dad apparently decided that the roof was again shipshape and began gathering up his tools. He could still see me sitting in the shade in the corner of the yard, and I guess that he thought Joe was there too, because as he neared the edge of the roof, he tossed down his hammer.

At that very instant, Joe was coming back around the house and the hammer hit the ground at his feet, barely missing him. He stopped, looked up, looked at me, grinned, then wheeled and ran into the house. In about five seconds he came running out with a bottle of catsup. He stopped by the porch, dumped the catsup

Joe, all scrubbed for church.

on his head, sat the bottle down and went over and stretched out in the yard, face down, with his catsup-stained head next to the hammer.

The roof was high, the ladder was long, and I was speechless. As Dad placed his foot on the top rung, he looked down.

No doubt thinking he'd mortally wounded his youngest son, his feet touched no other rungs.

As Dad's feet struck earth, Joe jumped up and ran. All this took place in a matter of seconds and I had no time to do anything, except the wrong thing, which was to start laughing.

I guess Dad knew that he'd been had and since Joe was long gone, he turned to me and I could see that he was angry.

As I rolled in the grass, laughing uncontrollably, he said, "Go in the house."

Now, one thing about Bill Pack was that he never whipped his children in public. I knew right then that I was in trouble and should not be laughing because it was the witness, not the perpetrator, who was about to be the recipient of an angry father's justice.

Nevertheless, all I could do was laugh harder because I really thought that I had witnessed one of the funniest scenarios I had ever seen in my life. How Joe had come up with this so quickly left me completely amazed—and in a heap of trouble.

Of course, the harder I laughed, the angrier Dad became.

"Go in the house!" This time he was more emphatic.

I finally managed a feeble, "I didn't do it, Daddy. Joe did it."

"Go in the house!"

I did. I met Mom in the kitchen and, still laughing, was trying to explain what I'd done, or in this case, hadn't done, when Dad walked in with a limb from the very tree that had been shading me as I watched him work on the roof, and a near-empty catsup bottle.

He looked at Mom, the catsup bottle, then at me.

"Where'd Joe go?"

I told him I didn't know, but I'd be glad to try to find him.

Dad looked at the catsup bottle again and kind of grinned.

"You ought to be more careful, Willie," Mom said. Then she started laughing, too.

Up to that very second, I sure thought I was a goner. I guess, though, Mom's laughter kind of broke the tension and after he thought it over, I suppose Dad realized just how close he'd come to braining Joe and thought better of doing the same to me.

Joe must have eventually returned home for he still lived with us when I left home for college. If Dad ever punished him for scaring him half to death, I wasn't aware of it.

• • •

I doubt seriously that all the disciplinary actions ever administered by Mom and Dad could have even come close to what I really deserved, but on those occasions when I *was* in trouble, my young heart was filled with fear and dread for as high as three or four minutes at a time.

Parents back then had a way with kids that modern parents do not have. Too many psychology books have taken the sting out of parental discipline. When I was in hot water with Mom or Dad, a gentle tap from a slender willow limb around my bony bare legs was more than enough to get my attention and correct any immediate problems.

But, being as clever as I was back in those days, I was soon able to recognize the "danger signals" and thus learned to avoid many a licking. For example, when Mom yelled for me to come home, and she used my full name, I knew I was in deep trouble. Mom never called me by my full name unless she was upset. When she said, "*Clyde Roy Pack*, you get to this house right now!" I knew I'd had it. And when Dad yelled, "Clyde," followed by, "Come a jumpin'," the red flag went up. I took proven scientific action in those cases: I'd find a flat rock and gently lift it without disturbing anything around it. Then, I'd spit under it and place it back, just the way it had been. If I could manage to do this, my punishment would never be severe.

• • •

And then there was Little Cecil. He was a bit younger than Joe and was kind of a loner. By that I mean he seemed to prefer playing by himself rather than join the group for a round of kick-the-can or cowboys and Indians. Everybody seemed to like him, though.

He's the only Cecil I knew, except Archie VanHoose's Henry Cecil, and *Little Cecil* wasn't him. Since he wasn't little, I can't imagine the need for the "Little" part in his name. Of course, that wasn't all that unusual because there was also Fat Mitchell Castle who was the *only* Mitchell Castle I knew, and Little Bill Puckett, was the only Bill Puckett I knew.

Anyway, Little Cecil loved cats but was extremely hard on them. He really didn't mean to, but it seemed he mangled, crippled or killed every cat with which he came into contact. Therefore, since his reputation was well-known to all, it's quite natural that he was brought into contact with the butterscotch-and-white stray kitten that we had designated as the recipient of our next funeral service.

Bear in mind that when we were seven or eight years old in Eastern Kentucky in 1946, we didn't have such diversions as video games or Trivial Pursuit. We were, however, blessed with very creative imaginations and we knew how to have fun.

For example, when the two-week revival was held every summer at the Thealka Free Will Baptist Church, the boys and girls in Society Row would attend the services, take mental notes and replay them the following day. When my cousin J. B. Castle (he was Mom's half-brother Henry's son), who was about my age, was visiting from down on White House, about half a dozen of us dammed up the creek at the culvert beneath the big sycamore and baptized him. We held him under until he bubbled, and when he came out yelling and screaming, we all whooped and shouted right along with him. It was a spirit-filled baptism and we didn't realize he was really mad until he had three of us whipped.

Anyway, when the make-believe preacher asked if any one else wanted a dunking, no one else did, so the services were over.

"Now what?"

"We've had a baptizing. Now let's have a funeral."

"Who's dead?"

"Not a real one, Dummy, play like."

Right on cue, the butterscotch-and-white kitten came from the dairy barn and walked right up to us.

"Let's bury that cat. It ain't nobody's."

"Let's kill it."

"We can't kill it."

"Little Cecil can."

"He won't, though."

"Yes he will, he just won't mean to."

We found Cecil sitting on his back steps breaking the heads off kitchen matches, putting them on a piece of T-rail and hitting them with a hammer.

"Here, Cece. We had this contest and you won. You won this cat."

His prize seemed to tickle him to death. As he walked through the neighborhood proudly carrying his new pet by the throat, I smiled and said, "Let's dig the grave, boys."

In less than two hours, not only had we dug the grave, but we'd also found a fairly new shoe box to use as a casket and a big roll of miner's tape to fasten the lid on good and tight.

When we got to Cecil's house, even we were surprised to see the shape that poor cat was in. The hair on its back was all gapped, one of its eyes was puffy and swollen and its tail was bent. It looked like it had been run over by a lawn mower.

"What happened to him, Cece?"

"Well, I didn't go to, but I run over him with the lawn mower."

"Well, he looks like he can't last long."

"Yeah, he's a goner all right. Might as well bury him."

The cat looked really awful, but he had a lot of fight left. I got scratched pretty good, but we got him taped in.

I don't mean to brag, but the service was beautiful. We preached that cat right through the Pearly Gates and then covered his grave with large rocks and wild daisies.

After the funeral, we drifted off in various directions in groups of twos and threes, each seeking a new distraction. It was about three hours later and nearly dark when J. B. and I finally got home. As I turned the corner of my house and started up the back steps, the butterscotch and white cat, the lawn-mower incident very much in evidence, stood up, purred, and rubbed lovingly against my legs.

I didn't then, nor do I now, believe in ghosts, be they human or feline. I'm not stupid, either, and to be on the safe side, I treated that cat with loving kindness. I kept him for several weeks; then one day I noticed he was gone, just disappeared.

Although I didn't dare mention it to anyone, I suspect he might have strayed over to Cecil's house.

• • •

The houses in Silk Stocking Row all featured a wooden walk leading up to the front porch. One day when I was coming back from the company store with a box of kitchen matches, I witnessed a sight the likes of which I'd never seen before: a grown man was walking on his toes.

I had been moseying along, kind of looking down at the ground and was nearly past the house when I saw him. But, sure enough, there he was, standing on one toe with his other leg sticking straight up.

Mom had taught me that it was ill-mannered to stare, so I sort of watched him out of the corner of my eyes as I walked by. When I got past him, though, I broke into a dead run. I had to tell somebody what I'd seen.

Mom was nowhere in sight so I left the matches on the kitchen table and headed for the rope swing in front of the dairy barn. There I found at least half a dozen listeners my own age. Joe was there, and Paul and Wib VanHoose and Libby Ann Green.

After I'd explained what I'd seen, one of them asked, "Was it down at Harry Thomas'?"

"I think so, I dunno, why?" I answered.

"Well, he's got this boy that's a toe dancer. He lives away from here, New York or California, or somewhere. That's been him you seen."

Well, at least he had been identified, but what he was doing was the strangest thing I'd ever seen.

About three or four days later, though, I had the opportunity to watch a more complete performance, and that's when I came to fully understand the fine art of ballet.

I was lying in my front-porch swing reading the latest issue of Captain Marvel when —Shazam—Paul VanHoose poked his head around the corner of the house and said, "He's doing it again."

"Who's doing what?"

"Harry Thomas' boy is dancing on his toes again! Come on."

We started down the road and Paul said, "Wait. Let's go down the back lane. He'll see us this way."

We did, and then cut through Lizzie Colvin's back yard, right next door to Harry Thomas'.

So, we crawled on our hands and knees along the fence that separated the two houses, then inched our way on our bellies until we could see the dancer through the tall irises that Lizzie had growing next to her fence.

As he walked on his toes and stuck his arms and legs over his head, I whispered, "I don't hear no music."

"He's just practicing," Paul whispered back.

"Well, he still needs music, don't he?"

"Maybe toe-dancing music is like a dog whistle."

"That's the dumbest thing I ever heard. Dogs can't whistle."

"I mean maybe he can hear it, but we can't."

"Maybe. I guess that's it." We lay in awe for several minutes, just watching.

"How on earth does he stand on his toes so long?"

"Look at 'em. Look how flat they are. He's had 'em chopped off. Anybody could do that if they chopped off their toes."

Suddenly, the dancer stopped dancing, turned and walked into the house, and I never saw him again for many, many years.

From time to time, we'd hear reports on how well he was doing; how he was dancing in a big Broadway show and how he was teaching ballet in New York. We even saw his picture once in *Look* magazine teaching Jane Fonda how to dance. More often than not, though, the reason his name popped up in conversation was because he's the father of Richard Thomas, the actor who played John Boy on *The Waltons*.

A couple of years ago, I stopped and chatted with that long-ago "toe dancer" on the steps of the Paintsville Post Office. When I told him of the first time I'd seen him do his stretching exercises he seemed amused.

As we shook hands and he walked away, I couldn't help but

feel that my conscience was cleared by my confessions of a time some 50 years ago when I became a spy.

• • •

On our way to becoming whatever destiny has mapped out for us to be, we all meet adults who, without our even knowing it, influence our thinking, help mold our character, and consequently become very dear to us. And, more often than not, we don't realize just how special those people are until we're well into adulthood ourselves. Such is the way I felt toward Lizzie Colvin.

Next to my own mom and dad, I don't know anyone for whom I had more respect, or whose advice I cherished more. I never called her anything but Lizzie. I doubt that she would have permitted me to call her "Mrs. Colvin" anyway.

Lizzie was a round little woman who always scurried wherever she went. I never saw her depressed and I'll always remember her make-believe threats whenever one of us would say or do something of which she disapproved: "Honey, I'll smack your mouth."

Lizzie Colvin.

When I was a boy, if I wasn't at home, nine times out of ten, I was at Lizzie's. Her husband, Ray, had died (I think of TB) in 1947 and her older children, just like my older brothers and sisters, were grown and had moved away. But her youngest daughter, Lois Ann, who was one grade above me in school, and her grandson, Tom "Tucker" Daniel, who was my age, lived with her, and we all walked to school together. Since I lived further on up the hollow, Lizzie's house was my first stop of the day. Lizzie had become an institution in Muddy Branch, and was the community's resident historian, record keeper and chief adviser.

She lived well into her nineties, and during one of the last conversations I had with her, she reminded me of the time that she was a substitute teacher at the H. S. Howes Community School when Tucker and I were in about the fifth grade.

Since I had been to her house hundreds of times and she had even fixed me fried chicken for breakfast once, it was quite natural for me to assume that when she told the class to sit down, be quiet and get to work, she wasn't talking to Tucker or me.

After everyone else had settled down and gotten busy, the two of us sort of meandered back to the cloakroom to perform whatever evil deed we had in mind at the time. (Tucker remembers that there were some girls involved, but he surely must be mistaken.) Anyway, Lizzie followed us. Someone must have hidden the teacher's regular paddle for what Lizzie held in her hand was a piece of desktop about five inches wide, twenty inches long and an inch thick.

Lois Ann Colvin and Tom "Tucker" Daniel.

There we were, cornered like rats in that cloakroom. She began swinging that piece of lumber with reckless abandon, and how we ever escaped with just a swat or two is a downright miracle. For the rest of her life, I accused her of trying to kill us that day. She'd just laugh, but never once did she deny it.

When I was a senior in high school, I sat at her kitchen table and told her I was thinking about going to college. I'll never forget what she said: "Son, you go if you can. You'll make something out of yourself."

Well, I suppose her prediction still remains to be seen, but I'll always appreciate her words of encouragement.

Any memory of what was good in those days always includes thoughts of Lizzie Colvin.

• • •

Then there was "Booten."

That's what we all called him (I've no idea why), and at the time none of us knew, or cared, for that matter, that the old gentleman who lived with Bill and Irene Hampton was really Irene's uncle, and his real name was Kanawha Puckett.

All we knew was that he was a friendly old man with a shuffle-foot limp who always had something clever to say and who could rid anybody he wanted to of warts. Some called what he did "charming" the wart, but we just said he was "trying on it."

The beauty about Booten's cure for warts, though, was that he'd nearly always accompany his treatment with a riddle or rhyme. While he was trying on the wart, he'd say something like, "I'll rub this wart and away it goes, be glad it's not growing on your nose."

I don't know what the poetry had to do with it, if anything, but it didn't matter whether his patients were young or old, they nearly always got a sample of Booten's rhyme.

Doctors say that warts are a kind of skin infection caused by a virus. Over the years, however, those who lived at Muddy Branch developed some extremely nonmedical cures for them.

For example, one old superstition that floated around among those who didn't believe in Booten stated that if you stole a dish rag, rubbed it on your wart, and then hid it, the wart would go away.

Another suggestion promised that sleeping with a piece of salt pork on your wart was supposed to make it go away. Still another that some older folks recommended directed the sufferer to tie as many knots in a string as you had warts. Then you were to hide the string under a rock. When it rotted, the warts would be gone.

I would suspect that every family in the camp had its own sure-fire, can't-miss cure for warts, and I'm equally certain that they all worked. But when I was growing up, Booten was the only cure I ever needed.

• • •

Come to think of it, when it came to cures, coal-camp families had one for nearly every ailment that came along. Here are a few that were passed around Muddy Branch.

- Cure yellow jaundice by drinking a tea made from the scrapings of a cow's horn.
- Heal a sprain by making a poultice from oil fried from the yolk of a boiled egg.
- Cure a headache by combing your hair. If any hair comes out take it outside and put it under a flat rock.
- Avoid headaches altogether by wearing rattlesnake rattles as a hair piece or by placing a piece of the snake root plant under your hat.
- Cure an earache by putting a few drops of whiskey or catnip in your ear. Earaches can also be cured if someone blows tobacco smoke into your ear.
- Relieve pain from a minor burn by applying foam from a pot of soup beans.
- "Break out" measles by drinking tea made from sheep manure or by putting burned cornmeal into a tobacco sack and tying it around your neck.

- Cure the croup by drinking juice from a baked onion or rubbing the patient with oil rendered from skunk fat.
- Cure cramps in your feet by turning your shoes upside down before going to bed.

Folks were also big on superstitions in those days.

- If a girl spills flour while baking, her future husband will be a drunk.
- If you find a snail on May 1, put it down in some sand and it will write out the name of your true love.
- If you start on a journey, it is bad luck to go back home unless you turn your cap around.
- It is bad luck to have two clocks running in the same room.
- If a man has never seen his father, he can draw fire from a burn by simply blowing on it.
- The higher the hornets build their nests, the higher the winter snows will be.
- If it thunders in February, it will frost in May.
- If it rains on Easter Sunday, it will rain for the next seven Sundays.

• • •

While we in Eastern Kentucky do indeed have a culture that is solely our own in many respects, I've discovered that some of our ideas are more universal than I first imagined. For instance, I was discussing some old-time remedies with an old gentleman who grew up in east Texas, and he told me that when he was a boy his mother would soak a piece of bread in a saucer of milk, then apply it as a poultice to ease the pain of a minor burn.

I told him that our primary treatment for such an affliction was a paste made from baking soda and water. But, quite naturally, the conversation then turned to bread and milk as a meal. That's when I quickly learned that he too had enjoyed that combination, as he put it, "many's the time."

For some reason, I'd always thought that milk and bread was strictly ours, and it's funny, but I can't recall eating milk and bread except in the winter time. I can't imagine why it should have been considered a cold-weather meal, like vegetable soup or chili, but I can still see Joe and me huddled in front of the open-grated fire, each with a big bowl of cornbread and buttermilk cradled in one arm as we shoveled it in with the other.

I don't know about Joe and the man from Texas, but to this day I still love to crumble cornbread into a glass and cover it with ice-cold buttermilk.

Another thing the old Texan talked about was how much he enjoyed rabbit hunting when he was a boy. He said he ate an awful lot of rabbit when he was growing up. That, like the milk and bread, sounds a lot like Eastern Kentucky, too. Dad loved to hunt squirrels and rabbits and kept an old .12-gauge shotgun standing in the corner near the head of his bed.

Ernest hunted with it sometimes, but Joe and I were strictly forbidden to handle it and Dad even kept the shells on the top shelf of the hall press thinking we didn't know where they were, and even if we did, we couldn't get to them. Sometimes, when I was eight or ten years old, I'd sit on the edge of Dad and Mom's bed and play with the shotgun, break it down, and pretend to load and shoot it. I wasn't shooting at squirrels and rabbits, though. I was shooting bank robbers and various other crooks who roamed the West. I was a teenager, however, before I ever actually shot the old shotgun.

. . .

Another older person, by at least two years, who created havoc in the far recesses of my overactive imagination was my cousin Billie Jean McFaddin, my Aunt Goldie's girl. Of all the cousins I had on Dad's side, she's the only one I can ever remember coming to our house on a regular basis.

As I've said, I didn't then nor do I now believe in ghosts, but when Billy Jean would come and stay all night, (she lived on Hen Cliff in Paintsville) Joe and I always heard one fine ghost story before we went to bed.

She was a truly gifted story teller and could make haints, spirits and things that go bump in the night so real that we could reach out and touch them.

While the rest of the house snored away, I'd lie there staring at the black ceiling, listening to the old house do its thing. (And, as anyone who has ever lived in a Northeast Coal Company house can tell you, they could really put on a show.) Anyway, I'd imagine every figure, shape and form as the cause of every little squeak and rattle. Thanks to Billie Jean, many's the time I'd still be awake when Dad would get up at 4:30 to go to work.

. . .

I was more fortunate than many of my peers when I was growing up because I had a real-life, flesh-and-blood hero. Even though Ulysses and Hubert were in the Navy and fighting in the Pacific, the one individual I looked upon with awe, wonder and admiration, although I doubt that he ever knew it, was my other older brother Ernest, who was nine years my senior. He stood just over six feet tall, was skinny as a rail and had dark, thick brown hair that he parted and combed back in a

Hubert.

high pompadour over his forehead. By everybody's standards, he was really a handsome young man.

I suppose there were two main reasons that I admired him more than anyone else I knew, the first being his courage. I thought he absolutely had to be the bravest person who ever lived because he could, and would, catch snakes. Now don't ask me why a rational 15-year-old boy would do such a thing, but he did. Many times I came upon a crowd of 12 or 15 kids, mostly girls, in the neighborhood "ooohing" and "aaahing," and occasionally screaming as they surrounded Ernest, who, leaning against a fence post in the head of Society Row, as cool as a cucumber, let a yard-long blacksnake slither up his arm and round his shoulders and poke its head down the collar of his shirt.

More than once, too, I attempted to use *his* bravery to further *my* interests as it regarded making a good impression.

"No, Clyde. You can't go with us to the Red Jacket Rocks. You're too little. You can't keep up. You'll get hurt."

"Oh, yeah?" I'd say. "Well, I'll have you know that my brother Ernest catches snakes."

"Oh really? Wow! Well, come on ahead, then. You can be the leader," is what they'd never say, although I really expected them to.

Ulysses.

What they'd really say was, "So what? They're just black snakes or green snakes. They ain't poison or nothing."

"Well," I'd say, "that's just 'cause they ain't no poison ones around. Show me a poison snake, and Ernest'll catch him."

I really believed that, too. And furthermore, I really didn't care if they were impressed or not, because I was and that's all that mattered in the long run, I guess.

Reason number two for my considering Ernest a genuine hero was that he was considered by everybody to be the best swimmer in all of Muddy Branch.

There wasn't a mom in the whole camp who would even so much as hesitate to let their kid go swimming if they knew that Ernest was going. They trusted him completely.

Ernest was the best diver around, too. He'd make hardly a ripple as he'd spring from the home-made diving board, his skinny body knifing beneath the algae that adorned the surface of the Number One Pond.

Mary Jean and Ernest at the Number One Pond, 1948.

And, if that weren't enough, he was the only person I knew who could "get bottom."

He'd swim to the middle of the pond and disappear. Thirty seconds...a full minute...a minute and a half...two minutes later he'd resurface, his hands filled with thick, black mud from the pond's bottom, 20 feet below.

To me, it might as well have been 200 feet. As far as I was concerned, it was a remarkable feat, and he sure was really something.

• • •

When Ernest died in Texas, Ulysses and Mary Jean were with his family and agreed that at the end his courage remained intact.

Somehow, I'm not surprised. Once a hero, always a hero.

Ernest, 1990.

CHAPTER X

Oh, to be a Cowboy

Regardless of what else was going on in my life, nothing short of death or some natural disaster kept me from going to the movies. Had I lived twice, or even three times, as far from town, there's not a doubt in my mind but that I'd still have gone to the show every Saturday morning because I really loved my cowboy heroes. As a matter of fact, until I was about ready to go into high school, I wanted to be a cowboy. Which, I'll admit, was kind of strange given the fact that I'd never ridden a horse in my life.

But I stood in line on Saturday mornings waiting for the movie house to open. I was willing to lay down my dime (nine cents, actually), and Roy, Gene, Hoppy and the Durango Kid were willing to lay down their lives. I knew, without doubt, that my cowboy heroes would do whatever was necessary (and fair) to protect all the nesters and sod-busters from the likes of those ugly bad guys who wore black hats, string ties and thin mustaches.

Have things changed, or what? I mean, when Randolph Scott played the town marshal and told the poor old widow Jones that he'd guard her money, she (and I) knew it'd be guarded. Today's hero, though, might just as easily shoot the widow, kidnap her niece, steal her buckboard and ride off on a big spending spree, with the audience cheering him on.

Furthermore, there were several other concepts of the old western that just wouldn't wash today. For example, people didn't bleed back in the forties. I sat for years and watched fist fights and gun battles and never saw ten drops of blood. Today's audiences would never accept bloodless violence.

I doubt, too, that today's movie-goers would accept the simple scenarios that we did. Like when the good guy, nearly always on the white horse, chased the bad guy, nearly always on the black horse, we knew he'd never catch him and knock him off his horse until they came to a little hill over which they could both roll. Even we had sense enough to know that if they'd hit the flat ground, it would have killed both of them.

And would folks today accept rocks big enough to hide a 40-piece orchestra? How many times did we see Gene and Old Frog Milhouse break into song as they rode alone across the vast prairie, only to be accompanied by orchestra music? If the musicians weren't behind a rock, where in the world were they?

"Yeah, they were behind those big rocks," we'd agree as we walked home after the show.

Back then, when a villain was finally headed off at the pass and toted off to jail, and when the hero patted his girl on the head and kissed his horse and rode off into the sunset seeking yet another wrong to right, we all headed for the popcorn machine. Now, though, we must sit and listen to the hero explain to his sidekick why the crook was a crook and how he was misunderstood as a youth and how he turned to a life of crime only after being falsely accused of robbing Wells Fargo when he was just a mere boy of ten. Before he's finished, we're all disliking the hero who caught him and feeling sorry for the crook.

We didn't care that the cowboy films were child-like, because that's what we were. But today, I don't enjoy the so-called adult westerns.

• • •

For a quarter we could go to both theatres on the same day (the Sipp first, then the Royal) and still have enough for a seven-cent root beer from the Royal Theatre fountain, where sister Mary Jean worked for a while.

On any given Saturday, we could see four features, two sets of previews, two cartoons, two cliff-hanging serials, and two versions of the news of the day. On Sunday each theatre ran one long feature. Both ran double features at night during the week but I seldom went to those.

Actually, if you counted all the double features that ran at the Cain Auto Drive-In, adults at that time had access to 25 or 30 movies a week.

Movie-going was a serious business in those days, as was

The Sipp Theatre in Paintsville, Kentucky, as it looked on those Saturday mornings in the late 1940s. Admission for a double feature was nine cents.

emphasized by some ads I came across recently in 50-year-old copies of *The Paintsville Herald*.

• When *She Wore a Yellow Ribbon*, starring John Wayne, ran at the Sipp on April 2 and 3, 1950, the following announcement accompanied the ad: *"The first 25 women in line wearing a yellow ribbon in their hair will be admitted free."*

• In January 1951, the ad from the *Herald* for the Royal featured *Desperadoes* starring Randolph Scott, *The Fuller Brush Girl* starring Lucille Ball, and the following announcement: *"Lost and found department—We have one boy's raincoat, one boy's corduroy coat, one boy's poplin sport jacket, one long black jersey glove, lady's— Found Sunday night, one pair wool gloves, girls'. We have a lot of other articles such as boys' and men's pocketbooks, girls' pocketbooks, scarves. If you lost anything, check with us. We may have your lost article."*

• In December 1950, the Royal Theatre also ran this statement: *"We regret the time has come when we are compelled to make a change in our admission prices. We are proud that we have been able to maintain minimum admission prices, increasing our price only four cents during the past ten years.*

"Every item of operation, such as wages, supplies, advertising, state and city license, taxes, changing to first run policy, etc., have increased to such proportions that we can no longer absorb this increase. Therefore, we are compelled to make the following changes in our admission prices. Matinee: Children, 12 cents, plus 3 cents tax, total 15 cents. Adults, 23 cents, plus 7 cents tax, total 30 cents. Night, Children 15 cents; Adults, 31 cents, plus 9 cents tax, total 40 cents."

That announcement probably did little to curtail my movie

going since it would take only another nickel to get me into both shows. I don't know how I managed to swing the other seven cents for the root beer.

• • •

A few years ago as I had my morning coffee, I picked up the *TV Guide*. The entry that caught my eye simply read as follows: "Movie, Western, BW; 90 min. 'Silver Canyon.' (1951) Gene Autry."

As an old-western fan, this looked like a winner to me.

It wasn't.

What I expected was a little escapism entertainment, perhaps a trip down memory lane. What I got was a swift kick of betrayal and yet another reminder of my own mortality.

The film was scheduled for the middle of my working day, and as I set the VCR I couldn't remember whether I had already seen this one. However, I thought that chances were pretty good that I had, because when I was a kid growing up, few of Autry's films escaped me.

As I looked over, under and around my trifocals trying to program the proper time, channel and length (the last time I had attempted this I had ended up watching Julia Child filet a chicken), my mind raced back to those days when I would dig the nine cents admission from the pocket of my jeans, buy my ticket, enter the old Royal Theatre and watch my old saddle pal round up the bad guys on a typical double-feature Saturday.

Not being as sophisticated then as I am now, it didn't matter to me that old Gene wasn't really much of an actor and his lines were delivered as if they were being read. I didn't care that his films were not really in black and white, but always had a pinkish cast to them, and it didn't bother me in the least that the plots in all his films were predictable and contrived and I always knew what was going to happen before it did. All I cared about was that Gene was just another of my many cowboy heroes who always triumphed over evil. His sidekicks, Smiley Burnett or Pat Buttram, would provide the comic relief and all I had to do was sit in the dark and watch.

Anyway, a couple of nights after I'd taped "Silver Canyon," I talked Wilma Jean into fixing some popcorn and, with a big diet 7-Up, I played the tape back. I had programmed it correctly. I now wish I hadn't.

The show was called "Melody Ranch Theater," and as the introduction ran, there were Gene and Pat Buttram—just like they were back then, in living black and white—smiling, waving and looking invincible.

Then, the program suddenly changed to color.

The Gene Autry in my memory was of the 1940s and 1950s, just as he had appeared at the top of this show. The Gene I now looked upon in horror was of the 1980s. He was dressed in a powder-blue suit that was at least two sizes too small. He sat in front of a painted window talking to an aged Pat Buttram, who also looked poured into his cowboy suit. As they sat and chatted uncomfortably about the days they made "pictures" together, they both seemed to be straining for something to say and it was difficult for me to determine if they were talking about the same thing. Gene looked extremely weak and peered out of eyes that seemed too small for his face and it seemed he was having difficulty whistling his words through dentures that didn't fit. The only remotely familiar thing about the old gentleman was his big white hat and the distinctive way he wore it.

I felt sadness. I felt betrayal. I felt disappointment. Autry had had an opportunity for immortality, at least in my mind, as his youthful image was forever committed to celluloid to be played back again and again.

When "Silver Canyon" finally came on, young Gene was on Champion riding along in front of a stagecoach singing. The last line of his song echoed in my mind: "I tell you folks it's Heaven, to be riding down the trail, when that evening sun goes down."

Why couldn't it all have ended like this particular movie had begun? Time had really done a number on old Gene.

Then it hit me.

Time had really done a number on me, too.

• • •

After spending week after week enjoying those double features, everything Gene did looked so easy and appealing to me. But, when I was about 10 years old, my attempt to mount a running horse was nothing less than disastrous.

Maybe the fact that I was unfamiliar with horses, and sometimes even a bit afraid of them, added to my failure. But for whatever reason, I have scars that I'll never show to prove that I was not a genuine cowboy.

Back then, the roads in Thealka were dirt (or mud, depending on the season), and the one in Society Row that passed my house ended abruptly with drawbars that bisected a fence that ran from the road to the top of the hill on both sides.

The acres and acres of this fenced-in property, known as Slaughter Pen Hollow, was then used for, among other things, a place to keep livestock. As a matter of fact, the Pack family kept a cow there.

On the particular summer day that I attempted my equestrian acrobatics, a couple of other adventure-seekers my age, namely Paul VanHoose and Tucker Daniel, and I discovered that Austin Daniels, who had recently moved his family into Society Row, had pastured his little brown pony in Slaughter Pen Hollow.

I don't know if the pony was old or just a special breed, but he moved awfully slowly and was so sway-backed that I actually thought his belly was going to touch the ground. We all knew that a real cowboy would never try to ride such a pitiful creature, but the three of us thought we'd try anyway, if we could catch him.

So, we borrowed a short rope that Milt Ratliff had left hanging in the old dairy barn and set out on our round-up.

Now, the trouble was that Sonny Stafford, an old gentleman who lived in town and always dressed in a suit and tie when he checked on his livestock, had recently unloaded about half a dozen high-spirited, full-grown, regular-size and mean-looking horses in there, too. They were easily spooked and it was very difficult to get close to them. As our luck would have it, that little brown pony stuck with them like glue.

Our strategy became to separate, or as Gene would say, "cut out," the pony from the rest of the herd. It took the better part of the morning, but we finally caught him sleepily grazing on the rich clover on the side of the hill and got between him and his protectors. We chased the other horses on up the hollow out of the way and finally got our rope on the pony.

Then, for some reason, we couldn't decide who would ride him first, so we decided we'd all three ride at the same time.

I was to be the third to mount, and having a flair for excitement, and the burning memory of how Gene had done it last Saturday morning, I decided that I'd stand on the bank above the path. As they walked the pony by me, I'd simply jump on behind them.

Bad idea.

As I stood positioned, ready to leap, I imagined myself in

black and white and wearing a ten-gallon hat. The smell of hot-buttered popcorn was in the air as Red Ryder and Little Beaver approached. Everything went well until they were about ten feet away. Suddenly, the pony started to run. I guess I panicked, because as it passed me, I jumped...much too hard and much too high. I sailed, slick as a whistle, over the pony's back and landed bottom first on a pile of rusty tin cans and broken, brown Clorox bottles. In the process of looking back and laughing uncontrollably, both Paul and Tucker fell off. My memory of them rolling in the grass and laughing so hard you could have heard them all the way to town, still raises my ire. Didn't they know I could have been killed?

By the time we'd caught the pony again, not to ride, but to get the rope off so no one would know what we'd done, most of my bleeding had stopped.

I decided right then, though, that I'd have been better off had I not tried to imitate Rex Allen and Sunset Carson and instead been one of the Dead End Kids.

• • •

But as much as I loved those old B-westerns, I could have been traumatized for life because one of them caused me to come very close to witnessing a real-life lynching.

It all started rather innocently, actually, when about a dozen of us were playing cowboys. More specifically, we were re-creating the latest western we'd seen at the Saturday matinee, of course. As usual, about half of us were crooks and the other half main players (that's how we referred to the good guys). Two brothers in the neighborhood, Rollie Jay and Lester Ray, neither of whom could talk plainly, and both of whom were frail specimens with extremely bad teeth, ended up on opposite sides of the law.

In the movie, some vigilantes had waylaid the bad guys and taken them to an old, dead hanging tree just outside of town and were going to "string 'em up," only to be stopped by the sheriff, who insisted that it wasn't fair to hang anybody before he'd had a fair trial.

We chased from one ridge to another, shooting and fighting from behind the trees and rocks and had finally worked ourselves to the vigilante part of the script. When it came time to string up the rustlers, we all gathered beneath the big elm tree that grew on the bank across the road from the old dairy barn, just below the drawbars.

The noose (an old sea grass rope that had once been a swing, much like the one that more recently adorned our big sycamore) was already tied to a stout limb, so after we tied Lester Ray's hands behind his back, we placed it over his head, and stood him on a pop case. (Naturally, we didn't have a real buckboard).

As we waited for the sheriff to appear and put a halt to our proceedings, the fight started. What happened was that for some reason, Rollie Jay suddenly, and without warning, just flat hauled off and kicked the pop case from under his cattle-thieving older brother and, really and truly, left him hanging by his neck, his feet only inches from the ground, for two or three seconds, until the rope broke.

As his feet touched solid earth, he screamed, "Ton! You Trazy?" and, obviously having no respect for the law, instantly tore into his little brother.

In reality, the fight didn't last over ten minutes, but at the time it seemed like hours that they rolled and scratched and cussed and bit and rolled some more.

We all thought they were only playing at first, but when we got to listening to what they were calling each other—the "tunny bits," "tit ashes," and "batirds"—we realized they were really serious, so we attempted to break it up.

The trouble was that when I tried to pull one of them off the other, the other got mad at me for treating his "iddle brudder" too roughly, and then they both jumped onto me. The fur flew for a minute or two, until the rest of them could untangle the three of us.

Anyway, it ended peacefully, with all of us, the good guys and the bad, joining together in perfect harmony as we washed the sweat and dirt, and yes, even a smattering or two of blood, from our bodies in the Number One Pond.

• • •

I'm not really sure why, but I guess of all the cowboys that paraded across the silver screen on those long-ago Saturday mornings, Roy Rogers was my favorite with Gene Autry coming in a close second.

I suppose that's why to this day I wear a Roy Rogers wristwatch that son Todd bought me for Christmas several years ago, and have a glossy, full-color, postcard-sized photo of Roy and Trigger, along with a miniature wooden horse shoe bearing the message "Happy Trails," on the wall next to my computer at work. Quite obviously, then, the news of his death put a damper on my day, much like the day I heard that Elvis had died, except different. Different, I suppose, because Roy and I went back quite a bit further than Elvis and I did. As a matter of fact, I couldn't have been more than six or seven when the bunch from Society Row, on those days it was too cold to walk, would pile into the car with Florence VanHoose (she was Paul and Wib's mother, and the only woman who lived in the neighborhood who could drive) for the 10-minute trip to the Saturday matinees.

Except on one occasion, I've never been west of the Missis-

sippi, and the only time I was ever astraddle anything even resembling a real horse was when Dad borrowed a pair of mules
to plow with and let me ride one and little brother Joe ride the
other from the garden to the barn. Yet, when I'd climb on Trigger (the smartest horse in the movies) and perch myself behind Roy, we became "co-kings" of the cowboys and purged
the entire west of all varmints, be they four-legged or two.

As far as I was concerned, Roy was the ideal main player; a
straight shooter possessing skill enough to shoot the bad guy's
gun instead of the bad guy himself. On those occasions when
he found it absolutely necessary to shoot the evil doer, Roy had
the uncanny ability to hit him where he didn't bleed. I even
enjoyed Roy's singing, but do confess that his musical inter-
ludes were the best times to make those trips to the conces-
sion stand or the rest room.

In addition to being a crook's worst nightmare, Roy also
provided us with everything we could possibly need to make
our life complete, selling us everything from Roy Rogers gui-
tars to Roy Rogers chow wagon lunch boxes to Roy Rogers flash-
lights. But what I enjoyed most was the Roy Rogers comic book
"on sale every week at your favorite newsstand for only a dime."

Although I'd never heard the term at the time, there's little
doubt that Roy Rogers became my role model. Strangely
enough, without my even knowing it, he remained so throughout the years. Even today I much prefer a grainy old black and
white Roy Rogers' movie to just about anything else on TV.

Over the past few years, about the only time I'd see him on
TV was when he'd be on one of the Christian networks, talking about his religious beliefs and professing his faith in God.

I always felt he was sincere, and consequently feel that he's
gone to a better place and will never again need to chase black
hats across a golden landscape. I've a feeling, though, he'll have
ample opportunity to sing.

• • •

When I heard that Gene Autry had died, I think I was affected to a lesser degree than when I had heard a few months earlier that Roy had passed away. Of course, Gene's death wasn't totally unexpected because only a day or two before he died,

The deaths of Roy Rogers and Gene Autry prompted my editorial "cartoons of tribute" in The Paintsville Herald.

I'd read in the newspaper that he was in critical condition in a Los Angeles hospital. There was more than that to buffer the shock of his passing, though. You see, in those days before TV, Roy and Gene had become symbols of everything good to me as I followed their exploits on a weekly basis. They were larger-than-life heroes to this coal-camp kid, and what they stood for was instilled in me as surely as if it had been tattooed onto my skin. I truly believed in the cowboy ideal. I knew that if I could live up to the "code of the west" established by Roy and Gene, I'd live a better life...forever. I guess it could be called "the white-hat syndrome;" but I believed that if I was a square shooter, I'd always win. I guess, therefore, I just didn't worry much about Gene's final destination.

Unfortunately, the demise of both, mere mortals after all, came at a time when the very ideals for which they stood also appear to be terminal. What an ironic twist of fate that America lost both men at such a time in our history.

It's sad, but it appears that Gene Autry and Roy Rogers both outlived the very ideals for which they stood. Even more tragic is the fact that with today's "in-your-face" athletes and "do-unto-others-but-do-it-first" politicians, nobody seems to wear a white hat anymore.

CHAPTER XI

That Old-Time Religion

With tunes like "Give Me That Old-Time Religion" echoing from nearby hills, in true Bible-Belt fashion, one of the most exciting community events (second only to the pie suppers held at the H.S. Howes Community School) was a baptism.

I say "community event" because practically everybody, church-goers and non-church-goers alike, seemed to forget (at least momentarily, anyway) the war raging in Europe and thus the absence of most of their young men between the ages of 17 and 30, and assembled to participate, or simply watch, the familiar religious rite.

Unless we were in the midst of an extended dry spell, in which case the services were held at the Number One Pond, most baptisms took place in the dammed-up creek that ran in front of the church. Children sat with their feet dangling over the edge of the bank and adults stood anywhere there was a place level enough for them to stand. Someone would begin, "Shall we gather at the river, the beautiful, beautiful river...," and knowing the words by heart, those who wanted to would join in.

Actually, there was little beauty to our "river," just a few unidentified weeds along its edge, now hidden by the 50 or so onlookers who filled the Sunday afternoon with song. It was the same "river" from which, Monday through Saturday, we'd take an old coffee sack, split it and seine for minnows and crawdads. It was the same "river" from which we'd drink if we got hot and thirsty from playing fox and hound or kick-the-can. But when the crowds would gather, as far as we were concerned, the now thigh-high-to-a-grown-man water was the mighty Jordan.

Most of the time, the baptism was the result of a weeklong (or longer) revival. And most of the time at least a dozen or more newly-saved (or back-sliding) Christians, after having been convinced by the word of God, or dragged from their pews kicking and screaming (the Free Wills have been accused from time to time of being overly persuasive), took the plunge, literally. Unfortunately, single baptisms, although equally important of course, at least to the one being baptized, seldom drew much of a crowd

Baptisms were common at the Number One Pond.

other than the family or a few close friends of the the one being baptized.

The Free Will Baptist Church was the only church this side of town and although no one ever told me so, to me it was the only church *anywhere.* Those congregations referred to as Methodists, Catholics and Churches of Christ were, as far as I was concerned, just other branches of the Free Wills and held to no theological (or political) differences.

Anyway, we youngsters thoroughly enjoyed a good baptismal service and perhaps without really meaning to, rated each immersion. It's not like we held up numbered cards like at the Olympics, but we'd say something like, "Boy, he really shouted a lot, didn't he?" Or, "Well, she sure didn't shout much."

"Yeah, that's the way she done the last time."

• • •

It seems that the story of my life revolves around my getting into some sort of trouble when I haven't done anything over which someone should be upset. Even the aforementioned revivals caused me grief once.

As impish as Joe and I apparently were, there was one place where we knew better than to misbehave, and that was church. Now, we may have gotten by with getting into a wrestling match and turning over Mom's churn or maybe having a mud fight using Mom's freshly washed bedspread that was hanging on the clothesline as a shield, but we just plain knew that we'd get a good dose of willow tea (a medicine brewed up when Dad or Mom would wrap a keen willow switch around our boney legs) if we acted up during church services.

Mostly, my memories of the Thealka Free Will Baptist Church are good ones. The sweet smell of Juicy Fruit mixed with furniture polish and just a dab of Evening in Paris perfume still lingers in the back of my mind, as does the good old-fashioned congregational singing.

However, there was one incident that occurred when I was about seven or eight that got me into all kinds of trouble, and wouldn't you know, I was completely innocent of any crime.

But, before I go into all the details, let me say right from the start that this is one of those tales that has been told and re-told so many times about me by older brothers and sisters, that it's difficult for me to know the difference between what I remember or what I've been told. I do remember, however, that what happened, however it happened, brought down Mom's wrath in such force that I'll never forget it for the rest of my born days.

Anyway, that summer, as usual, we were having a revival with a "big preacher from away from here." That always puzzled me in a way, because I always considered our own preachers as "big preachers," and I'm not referring to their physical stature, either. Don Fraley and James Lyons and Raymond Dale could preach hell and brimstone so real you could smell the smoke.

But my favorite was Charley "Rat" Bailey. Not only was he loud, but he was also extremely animated and had a habit of running down the aisles all the way to the back pews, jumping and kicking himself in his own hind end with the heels of his shoes as he did. His boisterous style nearly always brought high-pitched shouts of "Glory!" from the women (who waved a wadded-up handkerchief high above their heads) and a hardy "Amen!" from some of the brethren.

Anyway, the "big preacher" at this particular revival was Ted Green. I don't know where he was from, but without air conditioning, when he preached fire and brimstone, you could nearly feel it.

The church was not equipped with fans, except the funeral home kind with the little wooden, tongue-depressor-type handles, and it must have been 120 degrees in the building that night. I used to think that it was a state law that all revivals had to be held on nights that were extremely hot and humid.

But every pew was packed, and people, for the most part, didn't seem to mind the heat. Joe and I were doing fine as we sat, like the little angels we were, with Mom sitting between us. Dad, being a deacon, usually sat up near the pulpit with the preachers.

There were always lots of visitors who'd come to our revivals to hear these big preachers, and the lady who occupied the pew directly in front of us must have been one of them because I had never seen her before. Come to think of it, I haven't seen her since, either.

This lady was very...well, let's just say she was "heavy set." (Maybe 300 pounds worth of heavy set.) I had sat and watched the beads of sweat run down the back of her neck all night, and when it came time for the altar call, we all stood to sing.

When I stood, my eyes just came to the top of the back of this woman's pew, and I found myself staring, through no fault of my own, directly at her rear end. I'll never forget it. She was wearing a purple, silky-satin kind of dress with big red flowers on it. As I said, it was awfully hot, and she was sweating so profusely that her dress, was kind of gathered up and stuck, kinda to her. Well, really, more like kinda *in* her.

She looked very uncomfortable, so I, wanting to do the Christian thing, reached over the back of the pew and gently pulled her sweaty dress from her sticky backside.

It's still a mystery to me how such an act of kindness could otherwise be mistaken for anything else, but just as I began to pat myself on the back for a job well done, my mother's hand closed like a vise on my shoulder, and I looked up into the eyes of a woman who had once been my sweet, loving mother. She said not a word, but I knew she meant to do me bodily harm.

With "Ye who are weary come home" ringing in my ears and "I'll kill you when we get home" coming from my mother's eyes, I, like I usually did in such cases, panicked.

But wait! Bill Pack didn't raise any fools. What was it the preacher had said not ten minutes ago?

"If you sin, you must repent!"

Repent I did. I simply reached over the pew again and stuffed that sweaty, silky-satin dress back where it had been.

Needless to say, all my memories of the Thealka Free Will Baptist Church aren't pleasant ones.

• • •

Most of the time the reason Joe and I got into trouble in church was for giggling. And, at least until I helped the lady with her dress, my only act worse than giggling was yawning. And, although Mom usually sat between us, after sweating through two hours of hard preaching, both Joe and I, although we knew better, were subject to uncontrollable fits of both.

As one might guess, both afflictions were also quite contagious, yawning perhaps

Joe and me, as innocent as we looked, were constantly getting into trouble at church.

more so than giggling. Unfortunately, back in those days both giggling and yawning, especially if performed in the Thealka Free Will Baptist Church when Don Fraley was preaching, were terrible sins and usually resulted in a swat or two on our behinds as the four of us walked home. Sometimes, if we lucked out, a mere scolding would suffice, especially if the forbidden act had occurred early in the services and Mom had time to cool down.

Scoldings after nighttime services weren't really all that bad since we couldn't see the look Mom was giving us, nor could she see us if we smiled (an often fatal act if detected during daylight hours) during her tirade.

I read in the newspaper recently that yawning is merely a

method of self-arousal when it isn't advisable to fall asleep, like, for example, during a church service. In other words, yawning is a clever way for us to keep ourselves alert.

If that's the case, then, all that trouble we had over yawning in church was really unnecessary since what we were really doing was trying to keep ourselves alert so we'd not miss a single word of the preacher's sermon.

But, as is usually the case, all this information has come to light much too late to do either Joe or me any good. Nevertheless, I'm glad that I saw the newspaper article and have been vindicated, at least to some extent. Now, if somebody somewhere would only decide that giggling in church simply is the same as a strong "Amen, Brother," at least two of my childhood acts of sinfulness may not tend to condemn me.

• • •

Joe and I were big Sunday School attenders. I don't remember that much about it, except we were expected to stand up and recite a Bible verse every Sunday, right after we sang "Jesus Loves Me." Whoever the teacher called on first always said, "Jesus wept" (John 11:35), which was the shortest verse in the Bible.

On those occasions when I wasn't the first to be called, I had John 3:16 down pat: "For God so loved the world that he gave his only begotten son..."

Birthday time was fun at Sunday School because anyone having a birthday that week, regardless of their age, would walk up to the pulpit and drop a penny for every year they'd lived into a mayonnaise jar with a slot in the lid. As each coin dropped, all the various age groups would gather and count aloud, "One ... two ... three..."

I doubt this practice was based on any biblical principle, but I enjoyed it, nevertheless. I also enjoyed the little Bible card we'd get every Sunday. It featured a scene from the Bible on one side and a little story on the other. Sometimes they matched, sometimes they didn't.

• • •

The Thealka Free Will Baptists were foot washers, but for some reason, Dad and Mom would never let Joe and me go to one of the foot-washing services. They only occurred about once a year at what Dad called "sacrament meeting time," and were held about 30 minutes after the regular Sunday morning services were over.

What I know about foot-washing meetings is the result of only what I've heard...and a little boy's imagination.

As far as I could figure out, a pan of water was placed before a member of the congregation, who would take off his shoes and socks, roll up his britches' legs and let another member wash his feet. Then, someone would wash the feet of the member who had just washed someone else's feet. I don't believe that a man could wash a woman's feet, and vice-versa, but I could be wrong about that.

Anyway, one person didn't wash more than a couple of people's feet because from the size of the crowds that would gather at the church, if everybody washed everybody else's feet, church would have lasted for days.

I think that foot-washing time was the only time the Free Wills ever took communion. I can remember Dad buying grape juice and taking it to church.

After all these years, though, I still don't know why Joe and I—or any of the other kids in the camp—were not allowed to go to a foot-washing meeting. We might have really enjoyed it.

• • •

One would think that as a person gets older, he or she would have more pleasant experiences when it came to church going, but that's not necessarily so.

Strangely enough, even though Dad and Mom were Free Wills and I was, as they say, "raised in the church," I didn't become a Free Will Baptist. I became a member of the Meally Church of Christ when Wilma Jean and I were baptized on December 28, 1982. We are now members of the Highland Church of Christ in Paintsville. Yet, as the following incidents will show, going to church has not always been an easy thing for me to do.

For as long as I can remember, and even though I don't do it very well, I've enjoyed singing in church. Not solos, or anything, but just joining in with other members of the congregation and singing all those old hymns with which we've all become so familiar. After some of the things that have happened, though, I've started to wonder about congregational singing, or at least the "let's all stand and sing" part of it. Take, for instance, the time when a lady almost hanged me. Perhaps this would have been an appropriate action when I was a kid and probably needed hanging, but now? I mean, I'm talking about something that happened only a few years back.

We'd stood to sing. As the song ended, naturally, we all sat down. As I bent over to sit, my tie fell over the back of the pew in front of me. My sitting motion continued, but so did the lady's in the pew in front of me. Consequently, she sat...on my tie. I felt like some cattle rustler in an old B-western as the knot tightened around my neck.

Fortunately, she was not a big woman and before any real harm was done, I realized what had happened and managed to jerk free. Even though I could have been strangled, Wilma Jean laughed. She laughs at the strangest things.

She didn't laugh, however, on another occasion when great harm could have come to me because of my standing to sing.

We'd been late for church that day, and the only seats available were in the very back row. Now, they weren't your typical church pews. Instead they were four old-fashioned, wooden, school auditorium seats. You remember the kind: the ones with the fold-up bottoms that were connected to each other.

Somebody had rescued them from the trash bin of some old school somewhere and sat them in the back of the church, just in case they were needed sometime...like on that day.

Anyway, Wilma Jean, son Todd, a fellow worshipper named Gary Hall, and I were occupying these seats.

We'd stood to sing. When the song was over, we sat down. For some reason, I sat before the other three. Maybe I sat too hard, but for whatever reason, all four seats flipped over backwards. There I lay, flat on my back, my feet sticking straight up, right in the middle of the church service. This time Wilma Jean was too embarrassed to laugh. As a matter of fact, she just stood there staring at the song book. Todd, who was a teenager at the time, stared straight ahead, as if figuring, "If I don't look, it didn't happen."

Fortunately, Gary had the presence of mind to pull both me and the seats upright. Then on the count of three, we all four sat.

I don't expect to see warning labels printed on the backs of songbooks, but take it from me, standing to sing can be hazardous to your health.

CHAPTER XII

Respecting the Dead

Perhaps it's a sad commentary on my pre-teen youth, but when I look back to those days when I was nine or ten years old, I realize that the only two reasons I was ever allowed to stay up late was when Mom and Dad would let me go to Bill Hampton's on Saturday night to watch wrestling on TV, or when they'd let me, especially in the summertime, sit up with some-body dead. In those days, it was absolutely unheard of, and probably even considered to be un-Christian, to leave a body at the funeral home, and so when someone in the community would die, I would really feel important when I'd (uninvited) jump in and help the funeral home man unload those battle-scarred, wooden, fold-up chairs from the back of his pickup. As I'd set them around the walls in the bereaved neighbor's living room, I thought I was really something.

I can't imagine why Dad and Mom let me do it. I don't know if they actually thought I wanted to sit up out of respect for the deceased's family, or if they really knew that I was just looking for an excuse to stay up late. For whatever reason, though, they'd let me, and along about dark other boys and girls would start gathering. Talking about it now, more than 50 years later, it really sounds bad, even disrespectful. But I had no ill intent. It was simply something I did when somebody died, and there were probably as many reasons for doing it as there were kids who did it. One thing I always looked forward to was the food—the tables and tables of food.

Extra tables would have to be set up in the kitchen to hold it all, and women from as far away as Number Three and Greentown would bring in chocolate pies and cakes and tons of fried chicken and nearly always a baked ham. Sometimes they'd even bring in something sort of exotic. As a matter of fact, it was on such an occasion that I ate my first pimento-cheese sandwich.

Anyway, while the adults would sit around in the living room (or some other room adjacent to where the body was), we younger folks would congregate outside on the porch and steps. We knew enough not to make much noise, so while the folks inside would sing hymns and sometimes have an actual church service, complete with conversions and shouting, we'd quietly catch lightning bugs or play a subdued version of kick-the-can, between, of course, our visits to the kitchen via the back door.

By about eleven, or so, most of the grownups, except for the two or three men who'd planned to stay the night, would have all gone home. If I was lucky, there'd be a good storyteller or two among the grownups who'd stayed, and I'd, between visits to the kitchen via the back door, sit on the porch and listen through the screen door as they'd smoke and drink black coffee and tell tales of how it used to be before John L. Lewis.

By about midnight, our ranks, which at one time had swollen to a dozen or more, would have diminished to a mere three or four boys who lived really close, and we'd, between visits to the kitchen via the back door, sit and doze and wait for morning to come.

It wasn't something I talked about a lot, and it certainly wasn't something I looked forward to, but sitting up with the dead was just simply something coal-camp kids did back then.

• • •

I was reminded of all that a year or so ago as Wilma and I were driving home from the Huntington Mall. It was a Sunday afternoon and there was little or no commercial traffic (translated: no coal trucks), so we were moving south on U.S. 23 at a comfortable clip.

Somewhere near the Johnson/Lawrence County line, we came up behind a string of cars either completely stopped or moving about five or ten miles per hour.

"Uh-oh, there's been an accident," Wilma said.

She was wrong. As we rounded a little curve we saw that a funeral procession was creeping toward us, and those in cars in front of us had simply stopped or slowed down in respect for the dead. As a matter of fact, where the shoulder was wide enough, some cars had even pulled completely off the road.

I find it interesting that such traditions seem to have held firm, even if the funerals and burials themselves have changed. Perpetual-care cemeteries weren't common in the 1940s, and men from the neighborhood would dig the grave in either a family plot or the community cemetery, which more often than not, was located at the very top of a nearby hill. Six or eight men were then forced to carry the coffin a hundred yards or so straight up a hill to its final resting place.

Anyway, it was good to know that we Eastern Kentuckians still have respect enough for the dead at least to slow down, or even pull over and stop where possible, when we meet a funeral procession on the highway.

They didn't occur every week, not even every month, but it seems that when I was a kid, funerals were held much too frequently at the Thealka Free Will Baptist Church. And, as would be expected of two curious pre-teen coal-camp kids, Joe and I attended every one we could. Of course, we didn't go unless Mom did. I guess (and rightly so) she feared we'd do something stupid to embarrass the family if we went by ourselves.

Once in a while, one of Dad's fellow miners would be killed on the job and even if we hardly knew him, that always brought a prolonged sadness to the Pack house. It made us realize that Dad was indeed employed in the most dangerous industry in the world.

Sometimes the deceased miner would have kids who we knew at school and more often than not, a week or two later they'd drop out and move away. As an adult I've learned that during the 1940s in some coal camps, widows and orphans were forced to move out of company houses when a miner was killed, or even disabled to the point of no longer being able to work for the company. I don't know if that was the rule at Northeast.

During WW II, there were two or three boys from Muddy Branch who had been killed in the war and Joe and I attended their funerals. We even followed the body to the graveyard which was on the hill behind the H.S. Howes Community School. At military funerals they'd always play *Taps* at the gravesite and as those sad notes would echo across the hills and hollows, it would be so still you could hear your heart beat. Even the birds seemed to stop singing. I guess those kinds of funerals were the saddest of all.

• • •

I was probably about 50—which, as my dad would have said, was "a right smart bit ago"—when I first started paying attention to the obit pages in the morning paper. Perhaps there is really something to the old joke that if you don't find your name, you shower and shave and go on with your day.

But seriously, one of the things I've found curious is that many people I knew as a kid who have long since moved away, are coming back home...to be buried.

For some reason, after having lived in various parts of the country (the Industrial North in particular) for nearly half a century, families of the deceased are returning their loved ones to familiar surroundings. It makes you think that although, physically at least, they found themselves elsewhere, their hearts and souls were still residing in these mountains.

Former Kentucky Gov. Happy Chandler, speaking of these transplants, was once quoted as saying, "I never met a Kentuckian who wasn't going home."

There's little doubt that had not the jobs played out, had not the coal companies decided they'd taken enough of our natural resources, many of these families would never have left in the first place. Had there been ample employment available enabling them to put food on the table and clothes on the backs of their children, many of these families would still populate these hills and hollows.

So who is better off, those who went or those who stayed? Might as well ask which came first, the chicken or the egg. But if one gave serious thought to that question, there would probably be ample proof to support argument for both sides.

And we suspect that oft times those who stayed wished they'd gone and those who went wished they'd stayed.

When a Memorial Day morning finds a shiny new car bearing foreign tags parked in the head of a hollow on a gravel driveway, it's easy to understand how those who have taken root here might wish their life different. On the other hand, when the owner of that vehicle is having a morning cup of coffee on the front porch of the old homeplace, watching as spears of sunlight burn off the Mist that has wrapped itself around the hilltops like an old woman would wrap her shoulders in a shawl; when the song of a cardinal replaces the desperate wail of a siren; when the only odor comes from the wild honeysuckle vines that line the fence just beyond where Mom has planted marigolds in the old tire, who knows? Maybe he wishes he had stayed.

So, who's to say who is better off? It's curious, though, that after years of separation, we Eastern Kentuckians tend to all end up in the same place.

CHAPTER XIII

On Winters Past

Even though it meant that Christmas was very close, I used to absolutely hate the beginning of the winter season. Even now, when Eastern Kentucky begins to display its fall colors, I can't help but remember a time when those breath-taking hues were merely harbingers of winter's arrival. They still remind me of that time more than a half-century ago when I was generally very traumatized by wintertime.

It all goes back to those times when I was very small and would press my nose against the window pane and beg Mom to let me go out and play like the dozens of other kids in Society Row who spent those Currier and Ives-like snowy days riding their sleds or building snow forts.

It usually took the entire first half of the winter to persuade her to let me go and the last half for me to recover from the day of play. It was always a mystery to me how everyone else could wallow in the snow all winter making snow angels, but when I did, I'd spend the rest of the winter indoors, covered with Vick's salve, trying to ward off pneumonia. It just seemed that no matter how far I tucked my britches' legs into those four-buckle arctics, my feet would still get wet and I'd end up with a nose that ran like a sugar tree for months.

Even school wasn't much fun for me in the wintertime. Contrary to the old tale that everybody back then had to walk at least 20 miles (uphill, both ways) to get an education, I only had to walk about half a mile to get to the H. S. Howes Community School. That was plenty, though, for by the time I'd get there, I'd be more than ready to thaw out in front of the large, gas space heater around which a dozen or so of us would gather and chat and compare the depth of the snow in our yards, which, depending either upon our ability to lie or our inability to measure, could vary six or eight inches.

Anyway, every time I'd back up to the stove and get real comfortable, some big bully from the eighth grade would wander in and start making small talk. When he'd see the back of my pant legs starting to steam, he'd suddenly reach down below my knees and pull them forward and hold them, literally cooking my spindly calves, until I'd kick and thrash around enough to get free. Then, everybody would have a hearty laugh at my expense and tell me I couldn't take a joke if I got mad.

I nearly always came in last, too, in the snowball fights we'd have on the way home after school. In the first place, Mom made sure that I was always dressed in so many layers of clothing that I couldn't throw hard enough to hit anybody. As if that weren't enough, the same pant-leg-pulling eighth grader, or someone just like him, would always dip his snowball into a water hole and slam me round the side of the head with it.

Once, in an attempt to dodge such an icy projectile, I ran slap into the side of a parked C&O coal gon and cut a gash over my eye. Although the bloody wound left no physical trace, I'm afraid it did leave a nasty scar on my memory.

Wintertime and I disagreed to such an extent that even when Mary Jean would make snow cream, I didn't enjoy it. I was probably the only person on Earth to whom this happened, but I'd experience excruciating pain in the palate of my mouth every time I took a bite. Even today, I can't eat an orange slush lest the same thing happen.

However, as they say, time heals all wounds, and now I even look forward to winter, sort of. Since I'm not as susceptible to colds as I once was, and since I don't have to contend with a bullish eighth grader hurling balls of ice, my perspective has changed. Now I look forward to the first good snow to provide me the excuse to stay inside, build a nice fire and read Louis L'Amour.

Getting old does indeed have its advantages.

• • •

For today's young people, the change in the seasons simply means that football is gone and basketball has taken over. It didn't used to be that way. Although I'm sure there were other indications as well, I can remember that one sure signal of the change from fall to winter when I was a kid was the sweet smell of wood smoke, not from fires inside the houses, but from outside as water was brought to a boil in a number two washtub for scalding the hog so Dad and a few helpful neighbors (people used to help each other back then) could scrape off the hair on a crisp hog-killing morning.

My memories of hog killing are quite vivid, because to a five-year-old boy, there is something about watching the lifeless form of a 300-pound hog being hooked by its back feet and hoisted onto three-legged hangers by four or five grown men. I was gagged and amazed as its steaming guts would be dumped into a washtub. My experience was, to say the least, a strange mixture of excitement and dread. I wanted to watch, but at the same time, I was hoping that Dad would send me to the house. He never did. Since he'd been killing hogs since he was old enough to help, I suppose he never gave it a second thought.

But as much as I enjoyed eating the pork chops and ham

and freshly ground sausage, I think I also felt a twinge of pity for the hog. Furthermore, next to the dead mule I'd seen once at the Number One Pond, it was the biggest dead thing I'd ever seen .

Anyway, hog killing signaled a 100 percent certainty that winter was mighty close.

As falling temperatures settled in on Muddy Branch, that same smoky aroma lingered in the backyards of Society Row for a week or two longer as women in the neighborhood gathered in groups of twos and threes and talked and laughed as they rendered lard from the pork fat or made lye soap and sliced it into large slabs.

I'm afraid, though, that those days are gone forever, and it's really too bad that today's generation of young people can't experience some of those sounds and smells and feelings associated with the 1940s and that time of the year when fall would suddenly give way to winter.

• • •

The most important thing about winter then, and it still ranks pretty high on my list, was the sparkle of Chirstmas.

The first real lights I can ever remember adorning one of our Christmas trees were a set or two of those little multi-colored, candle-shaped ones that Mom had ordered from the Montgomery Ward catalog. They were filled with some sort of liquid that bubbled, and had to be perfectly vertical, which meant that some member of the family was always fooling with them.

"Does that look straight?"

"No, it's leaning to the left."

"How 'bout now?"

"Yeah, that's better."

It took 10 or 15 minutes for them to warm up, but boy, when those bubbles started, they were the prettiest things I'd ever seen.

I couldn't have been more than six or seven years old at the time, but I recall just sitting and watching those tiny bubbles form and rush to the top of the little tubes and disappear. Almost immediately, another little bubble would form at the bottom and the colorful process would start all over again.

Just like folks do today, everybody in Muddy Branch who had a Christmas tree back then (more didn't than did) placed them next to their front room windows so those passing outside could see them. Sometimes I'd go out to the road in front of the house and pretend I was a stranger who just happened to have noticed the lights in our window and think how they were the prettiest ones in the whole camp.

We also had a couple dozen of those extremely brittle (we broke at least one of them every Christmas), but quite shiny, ornaments that seemed to reflect the bubbles, too, and helped make the tree really sparkle. Some of the neighbors used angel hair on their trees, but Mom wouldn't because she said it was dangerous. I don't know if she thought Joe and I might eat it, or what.

Other than the tree and presents, I don't think we ever did anything out of the ordinary in the way of celebration at home. We had homemade candy and stuff, but we had that all year long. Much to the delight of her little brothers, Mary Jean was always making fudge or sea-foam candy or popcorn balls.

All that was more than half a century ago, but even today whenever I pass a house all decorated for the holiday, I keep my eyes peeled for those bubble lights.

• • •

When I was very young, I was given a part in the Christmas play presented by the Sunday School classes at the Thealka Free Will Baptist Church. For obvious reasons, at least to me, anyway, I was selected to play a wiseman, a role I kept for years. Consequently, I learned to point at (and follow) the star of Bethlehem with the best of them.

The script was always the same.

You'd get all these little boys to play wisemen and had them wear chenille bathrobes. Since boys in Muddy Branch never wore bathrobes at home, practically every wiseman chosen had a sister. Mary Jean's bathrobe was a little short on me, but hey, beggars can't be choosers.

The wisemen would march really slowly across a stage and point at this big pasteboard star being pulled by a pulley on a string. They'd go very slowly until they came to some more kids dressed up like cows and sheep.

Then, they'd stop near a doll in a pasteboard-box manger with hay in it and some more kids in bathrobes. There would be this little girl with a towel draped over her head sitting on her knees looking at the doll, and a boy with a long stick standing behind her. They were Mary and Joseph.

Fortunately, the older I got, the clearer the beautiful story became, and since Dad was a deacon, it wasn't long before I was keenly aware of the true reason for the season.

I like to think I still am, but at the same time, I still have enough little kid in me to enjoy the sparkle-and-tinsel part of it, too.

That's why I can't understand why some folks I know exchange and open gifts days, even weeks, before Christmas. By the time Christmas gets here, there's nothing left under the tree except a carpet full of pine needles.

That's not the way it is at our house, though. Ever since I

was a little boy, I've always loved the surprise factor associated with opening one package on Christmas Eve and the rest on Christmas morning. I mean, I absolutely do not want anyone to know, or even guess, what I've wrapped for them. Nor do I want to know what's wrapped for me.

I've even gone so far as to wrap a brick with a piece of jewelry so Wilma Jean wouldn't be able to figure out what she'd gotten by shaking the package. Once, after I began teaching, I bought Joe a watch and wrapped it in a shoebox. Curiosity got the best of him and when he was alone in the house one day, he sneaked and opened it. His attempt to rewrap it failed, however, and I figured out what he'd done. I returned the watch to the store and replaced it with underwear and socks. Needless to say, he was surprised on Christmas morning.

• • •

My memories of those Christmases of the 1940s are still vivid and very special to me. Some are school-related because, besides all the festive decorations in the hallways and classrooms, student gift exchanges were a chance for me to get an extra present or two.

One way we did this was to draw names. On the Friday before our Christmas vacation began, we'd bring in the gifts for the persons whose names we'd drawn and that afternoon the teacher would hand them out. No doubt she had an antsy group of pupils the first part of the day because with 25 or 30 brightly wrapped presents of all shapes and sizes, all costing under a dollar, piled under the scrawny pine tree with its paper decorations, it was difficult for us to really care about educational stuff.

No one enjoyed these days more than I, but seldom did I

fare well when it came to receiving presents at school. It seemed like all the other boys got such neat things: checker boards, pocket knives, yo-yos; however, I nearly always got a box of chocolate-covered cherries. No matter who got my name, I got chocolate-covered cherries. Now, don't misunderstand, I like chocolate-covered cherries. It's just that part of the ritual was to open your present so everyone could see what you got. If that little white box had been a giant magnet and the students iron shavings, it couldn't have attracted any more attention. I might have managed to eat one or two before someone would grab the box. By the time it got back to me, it would be empty.

I also looked forward to the gifts from Caney Creek College, located at Pippa Passes, Kentucky. I've no idea why they took it upon themselves to treat us every Christmas. At the time, though, I was glad they did.

Mr. Chandler, our principal, would carry in a big pasteboard box and count out the proper number of "boy" and "girl" presents. They were generally the same, except the girls got a set of jacks where we got a bag of marbles to go with the ruler, pencil sharpener, compass and protractor.

At home we always had a Christmas tree, and of course, the lights that bubbled and popcorn tinsel we'd strung ourselves. But, as I've said, the prevailing atmosphere of warmth and the true meaning of the holiday was very much in evidence, too.

In this regard, a Christmas memory that I still cherish is one where I got very little in the way of presents.

It came when I was about eight years old. Dad wasn't getting much work for some reason, but on this particular Christmas Eve, he was working and there was no one home with Joe and me except Mom. We kind of sat around doing those ordinary things like listening to "I Love a Mystery," or Randy Blake's "Suppertime Frolic" on WJJD in Chicago, until well after dark.

Then Mom gave us our gift: a genuine, imitation-leather, cowboy-style wallet that she had ordered from Montgomery Ward. I spent all of Christmas Day cutting pictures for the little plastic windows from movie magazines that Mary Jean had bought.

I doubt very seriously that the wallet ever carried a piece of real money, but no amount of cash could have bought the kind of warm memories it now provides: memories that make me glad I was a coal-camp kid.

About the Publisher

Incorporated in 1979 for public, charitable, and educational purposes, the Jesse Stuart Foundation is devoted to preserving the legacy of Jesse Stuart, W-Hollow, and the Appalachian way of life. The Foundation, which controls the rights to Stuart's published and unpublished literary works, is currently reprinting many of his best out-of-print books, along with other books which focus on Kentucky and Southern Appalachia.

With control of Jesse Stuart's literary estate—including all papers, manuscripts, and memorabilia—the Foundation promotes a number of cultural and educational programs. It encourages the study of Jesse Stuart's works, and of related material, especially the history, culture, and literature of the Appalachian region.

Our primary purpose is to produce books which supplement the educational system at all levels. We have now produced more than 100 editions and printings and we have thousands of other regional books in stock. We want to make these materials accessible to teachers and librarians, as well as general readers. We also promote Stuart's legacy through video tapes, dramas, and presentations for school and civic groups. In keeping with Stuart's devotion to teaching, the Jesse Stuart Foundation is publishing materials that are carefully designed for school use.

Jesse Stuart's books are a guideline to the solid values of America's past. With good humor and brilliant storytelling, Stuart praises the Appalachian people whose quiet lives were captured forever in his wonderful novels and stories. In Jesse's books, readers will find people who value hard work, who love their families, their land, and their country; who believe in education, honesty, thrift, and compassion—people who play by the rules.

Today, we are so caught up in teaching children to read that the process has obscured the high purpose. Children require more than literacy. They need to learn, from reading, the unalterable principles of right and wrong.

That is why Stuart's books are so important. They allow educators and parents to "kill two birds with one stone." They make reading fun for children, and they teach solid values, too.

In a world that is rapidly losing perspective, we must truly educate tomorrow's adults. We must prepare school children for responsible citizenship, so we need to provide them with beneficial reading material.

Please help us make others aware of the books and materials available from the Jesse Stuart Foundation.

For more information, contact:

Jesse Stuart Foundation
P.O. Box 669
Ashland, Kentucky 41105
(606) 326-1667

Internet address:
JSFBOOKS.com
E-Mail Address:
jsf@jsfbooks.com

About the Author

Clyde Roy Pack is an associate editor at *The Paintsville Herald*, where he also writes an award-winning humor column. He was an elementary and high school art and English teacher for 33 years before retiring in 1994. He lives in Johnson County, Kentucky.

Acknowledgements

Without really meaning to, I began writing this book in the mid-1980s in the form of a weekly column for *The Paintsville Herald*. It was to be a general interest piece, but as time passed, it turned into a flood of memories about my growing up in Thealka, Kentucky, in the hills of Appalachia during the 1940s and 1950s.

In the early 1990s, I decided to compile the columns—along with other things I remembered that weren't quite suited for the newspaper—into book form. But once I had a manuscript, I'd no earthly clue what to do with it.

Enter Dr. Linda Scott DeRosier, whose autobiographical *Creeker: A Woman's Journey* was published in 1999. At the time, I was retired from teaching and was working part-time at *The Paintsville Herald*. One of my job descriptions was "book editor." When her book found its way to my desk and I realized that the Dr. DeRosier who had written it was the same person I had known as Linda Sue Preston when we attended Meade Memorial High School together in the late 1950s, I called and congratulated her on her new book.

We talked about a lot of things, including Two-Mile Creek where she grew up less than a mile up the road from my wife Wilma Jean. In discussing her book, I also mentioned mine. She asked to see it and I obliged. Thinking it showed promise, she began making suggestions, and as I made changes, she, in effect, became my mentor...my cheerleader. Without her interest this book would no doubt still be gathering dust in some corner of my closet. I'll never be able to thank her enough for helping make this project a reality.

When I thought I had everything in pretty good shape, daughter-in-law Marcy—a copy editor by trade—agreed to read the book. It took her a while, what with her primary concern being the care of our granddaughter Alison, but she did read every word and made the corrections that, had they not been made, would have likely embarrassed me. So Marcy, too, gets a big thank you.

Many of the photos in this book were gathered by friends and family too numerous to mention. They, however, know who they are and I'll be forever in their debt.

And finally, I owe thanks to Dad and Mom, Willie and Julia Pack, for providing me with a childhood of which I'm proud to write. I think they would be pleased with what I've done.